Amateurs wishing to arrange for the production of I'LL DIE IF I CAN'T LIVE FOREVER must make application to SAMUEL FRENCH, INC., at 25 West 45th Street, New York, N.Y. 10036, giving the following particulars:

(1) The name of the town and theatre or hall in which it is proposed to give the production.

(2) The maximum seating capacity of the theatre or hall.

(3) Scale of ticket prices.

(4) The number of performances it is intended to give, and the dates thereof.

Upon receipt of these particulars SAMUEL FRENCH, INC., will quote the terms upon which permission for performances will be granted.

A piano conductor score will be loaned two months prior to the production ONLY on receipt of the royalty quoted for all performances, the rental fee and a refundable deposit. The deposit will be refunded on the safe return to SAMUEL FRENCH, INC. of all material loaned for the production.

A special cassette required for the ninth musical number "A IS FOR," in the first act, as originally used in the New York production, is available at a cost of $8.25, which includes first-class postage and handling. Remittance must accompany your order.

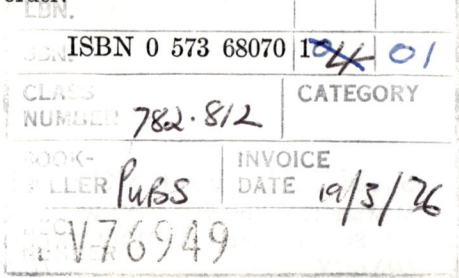

MUSICAL NUMBERS

ACT ONE

The Opening Number .... *The Company*
The Improvisation .... *The Company*
FLASHBACK:
Joys of Manhattan Life .... *Jonathan, Gabby, Ted*
Where Would We Be Without Perverts? .... *The Company*
My Life's A Musical Comedy .... *Gabby and Jonathan*
We're Strangers Who Sleep Side by Side .... *Jenette and Ted*
The Roommate Beguine .... *Heather and Dan*
A is For .... *Gabby*
Take Me! .... *The Company*
There's Always Someone Who'll Tell You "No" .. *Jonathan*
24 Hours from this Moment .... *The Company*

ACT TWO

THE REVUE WITHIN THE REVUE CONTINUES:
The Improvisation .... *The Company*
Ode to Electricity .... *The Company*
I'm In Love .... *Heather*
I'm So Bored .... *The Company*
My Place or Yours? .... *Jenette and Ted*
Who Do We Thank! .... *The Company*
Let's Have a Rodgers and Hammerstein Affair .... *Jenette,*
Heather, Jonathan and Ted
Less is More and More .... *Gabby and Dan*
I Hate Football .... *Jenette*
They Left Me .... *Heather*
It's Great to Be Gay .... *The Company*
I'll Die If I Can't Live Forever .... *The Company*
The Finale .... *The Company*
The Great White Way .... *The Company*

"I'LL DIE IF I CAN'T LIVE FOREVER"
a stage struck revue

Words, music, musical staging by *Joyce Stoner*

Additional music, musical direction and arrangements by
William Boswell

Book material based on a concept by *Karen Johnson*

Additional book material by *William Brooke*

Designed by *Irving Milton Duke*

Produced by *Patrick Stoner*

I'LL DIE IF I CAN'T LIVE FOREVER opened October
31, 1974, at the Improvisation, 358 West 44th Street, New
York, N.Y. 10036.

ORIGINAL CAST

DAN CRAIG	*Don Bradford*
JONATHAN WINSLOW	*Tom Hastings*
GABRIELLE SCHWARTZ	*Gail Johnston*
TED THORNTON	*Michael David Laibson*
HEATHER O'MALLEY	*Maureen Maloney*
JENETTE MORRISON	*Nancy Reddon*

Pianist—*Mark T. Long*

Stage Manager—*Dale Lally*

I'll Die If I Can't Live Forever

ACT ONE

The show takes place in the main entertainment room of a purposely tacky and junk-filled nightclub of New York City called "The Improvisation." Already twelve years old by 1974, this late night spot with its tiny stage has launched such notables as Liza Minelli, Dick Cavett, Bette Middler, Jimmy Walker, Freddie Prinze, Rodney Dangerfield, David Frye, Dustin Hoffman, Robert Klein, and Stiller and Meara. Everything has the appearance of being covered with years of dripped candle wax, caked plaster, and accumulated dust. Tiffany lamps hang askew from the ceiling, and brittle aged movie posters are precariously adhered to any available blank walls. The menu offerings are scrawled on a small blackboard with numerous corrections and erasures.

The six person cast files down the aisle in evening dress [contrasting sharply with the surroundings, which are strictly blue-jean] and proceeds to use every possible musical cliche staging technique on the postage-stamp stage as they sing:

(Lights, preset at half, come up to full.)

ALL.
THE OP'NING NUMBER, THE OP'NING NUMBER,
IT'S TIME TO START THE OPENING NUMBER.
THE CAST HAS ALL COME IN,
DETERMINED TO BEGIN;
IT'S TIME TO START THE OP'NING NUMBER.

THE OP'NING NUMBER, THE OP'NING NUMBER,
IT'S TIME TO START THE OPENING NUMBER.
IN SPITE OF COSTUMERS
AND CHOREOGRAPHERS,
IT'S TIME TO START THE OP'NING NUMBER.

7

MEN.
YOU WONDER NOW THAT YOU'VE ARRIV'D:
WOMEN.
HOW THIS LOCATION HAS SURVIV'D.
MEN.
WE'RE HERE IN EVENING DRESS
WOMEN.
AND READY, MORE OR LESS;
ALL.
A WAY TO START THE SHOW MUST BE
 CONTRIV'D!

ALL.
THE OP'NING NUMBER, THE OP'NING NUMBER
IT'S TIME TO START THE OPENING NUMBER.
THE GIRLS AREN'T DRESSED LIKE BOYS,
THERE'S NO ELECTRIC NOISE,
BUT WE WILL PLAY OUR PARTS
TILL THE FINALE STARTS.
HERE IT IS NOW: THE OP'NING NUMBER!

THE OP'NING NUMBER, THE OP'NING NUMBER,
WE HOPE YOU LIKE THE OPENING NUMBER!
WE'LL PROVE TO YOU IN RHYME
IT'S BUSBY BERKELEY TIME;
WE HOPE YOU LIKE THE OP'NING NUMBER.

JENETTE and HEATHER.
WE'VE BEEN REHEARSING QUITE A WHILE
JON and DAN.
TO SHOW YOU THAT WE'RE VERSATILE!
ALL.
WE'LL TRY TO ENTERTAIN
WITH EV'RY SONG REFRAIN,
AND HOPE THAT ONE OR TWO WILL MAKE
 YOU SMILE!

THE OP'NING NUMBER, THE OP'NING NUMBER,
WE HOPE YOU LIKE THE OPENING NUMBER!
AND NOW WE'LL DO SOME KICKS,
AND OTHER SIMPLE TRICKS;
WE'LL SING IN DIFFERENT KEYS
ATTEMPTING HARMONIES;
WE HOPE YOU LIKE THE OP'NING NUMBER!

THE OP'NING NUMBER IS ALMOST OVER
IT'S ALMOST TIME FOR US TO STOP SINGING.
AND JUST IN CASE YOU'RE BORED
IT WILL NOT BE ENCORED;
THIS ENDLESS SONG IS ALMOST OVER.

WE WON'T BE SAD WHEN IT IS GONE:
REHEARSALS LASTED TILL THE DAWN!
I THOUGHT THAT I WOULD DIE,
AND AT THAT MOMENT I
BEGAN TO WONDER "WHY SHOWS MUST GO ON!"

THE OP'NING NUMBER, THE OP'NING NUMBER
THE OP'NING NUMBER'S JUST ABOUT OVER.
THE SONG IS FINISHED NOW,
IT'S TIME TO TAKE A BOW,
WHICH WE WILL DO BECAUSE
WE HOPE TO HEAR APPLAUSE!
LET'S END THE OPENING, END THE OPENING,
END THE OPENING, END THE OPENING, END
   THE OPENING, AHHHH. . . .
END THE OPENING, END THE OPENING, END
   THE OPENING . . .
IT'S TIME TO END THE OPENING, END THE
   OPENING, END THE OPENING SONG!
IT'S TIME TO END THE OPENING, END THE
   OPENING SONG
IT'S TIME TO END THE OPENING SONG.

(*BLACKOUT.*)

(HEATHER, JENETTE, *and* DAN *are left onstage to serenade
   their surroundings . . . just to let their audience know
   they're aware of the unusual qualities of their "theater."*)

   HEATHER, JENETTE, and DAN.
NINTH AVENUE AND FORTY-FOURTH STREET!
FORTY-FOURTH STREET AND NINTH
   AVENUE-OO-OO-OO-OO!

HERE WE ARE AT THE IMPROV, THE
   IMPROVISATION!
WE'RE ABOUT TO PRESENT JUST ONE MORE
   MUSICAL REVUE.

HEATHER.
IT ISN'T THE PLAZA
JENETTE.
IT ISN'T THE WALDORF.
DAN.
IT ISN'T EVEN JIMMY'S
ALL.
BUT I GUESS IT'LL HAVE TO DO!

THESE BRICKS RESOUND WITH HISTORIES
OF FAMOUS PERSONALITIES
GIRLS.
MAYBE THEY'RE NOW ON THE
    ENTERTAINMENT PAGE . . .
ALL.
BUT YOU SAW THEM FIRST STRUGGLING HERE
    ON THIS STAGE

AT NINTH AVENUE AND FORTY-FOURTH STREET!

GIRLS.
LILY TOMLIN, JANIE SELL, AND LIZA WITH
    A ZEE-EE
PUT UP WITH THAT LADIES' ROOM, SO WHY
    SHOULDN'T WE?

DAN.
LEGENDS STILL HAVE IT
THAT EVEN DICK CAVETT
FELL ON HIS FACE IN THIS VERY SAME PLACE!

ALL.
LET'S HEAR IT FOR THE TACKY, KINKY,
    FUNKY, FADED,
HOLE-IN-THE-WALL AND JUNKY, JADED
IMPROVISATION!

HERE WE ARE AT THE IMPROV, THE
    IMPROVISATION!
WE'RE ABOUT TO PRESENT JUST ONE MORE
    MUSICAL REVUE.
HEATHER.
IT ISN'T THE UPSTAIRS,
JENETTE.
OR EVEN THE DOWNSTAIRS.

DAN.
WE CAN'T TAKE OFF OUR CLOTHES HERE
ALL.
BUT I GUESS IT'LL HAVE TO DO!

WE CAN'T REPRISE THIS SONG AGAIN. . . .

(*The three, still in evening dress, fade out to change into street clothes. This number returns in the beginning of the second act to re-begin the revue within the revue. We now flashback to find* JONATHAN, *arriving from Omaha at Port Authority, suitcase in hand, looking pitiful . . . Lights fade, spot up on* JONATHAN.)

JONATHAN.
LITTLE DID I REALIZE ALL THE WONDERS I
    WOULD SEE
AS I STEPPED OUT OF A GREYHOUND INTO
    PORT AUTHORITY . . .
I'VE LEARNED TO . . .

(GABBY *and* TED *enter, bump as hurried New Yorkers, fuss, and jump into simulated subway poses to sing:*)

ALL.
. . . LOVE EACH RIDE ON THE LOCAL I.R.T.
GABBY.
BUT OF ALL THE HANDS I'M FEELING ONLY
    TWO BELONG TO ME!
TED.
I RUSH TO CATCH A TRAIN WITH A TOKEN
    IN MY FIST . . .
GABBY.
I'LL NEVER LOSE MY PURSE BECAUSE IT'S
    PADLOCKED ON MY WRIST!
TED.
I LEARNED SUBWAY DECORUM, IT ONLY TOOK
    A WHILE:
YOU NEVER SAY GOOD MORNING AND YOU
    MUSTN'T EVER SMILE!
JONATHAN.
I'D LIKE TO MEET SOME NEW YORKERS; WISH
    I COULD,
BUT I CAN'T EVEN ASK DIRECTIONS CAUSE MY
    SPANISH ISN'T GOOD!

ALL.
BUT IT'S A JOY, JUST A JOY (YOU CAN'T
    IMAGINE)
ADJUSTING TO MANHATTAN LIFE!
GABBY.
I HAVE ADVENTURES HERE EVERY TIME
    I TAKE A WALK:
SUCH FASCINATING PEOPLE WANT TO STOP
    AND HAVE A TALK!
TED.
THEY GIVE ME FLOWERS OR THEY JUST WANT
    TO KNOW THE TIME.
JONATHAN.
THEY TRY TO SELL ME *ANYTHING* (*Prostitute pantomime.*) OR ASK ME FOR A DIME!
TED.
IT'S FUN TO WALK ON BROADWAY, WHERE
    FLASHING LIGHTS BEGIN . . .
GABBY.
BUT I'VE LEARNED TO BE QUITE CAREFUL OF
    WHAT BOOKSTORES I WALK IN!
TED.
I'M NOW SO BRAVE THAT NO LONGER I'M
    DISTURBED
AT SLIPPING DOWN THE SIDEWALK WHERE
    THE DOGS HAVE NOT BEEN CURBED!
ALL.
BUT IT'S A JOY, JUST A JOY (YOU CAN'T
    IMAGINE)
ADJUSTING TO MANHATTAN LIFE!

(*They cross the stage into an imagined apartment area.*)

TED. You must be the new tenant! I'm 4-E.
JONATHAN. Yes, I'm, uh, 3B . . . Jonathan to my friends.
TED. (*Shaking hands.*) Ted Thornton. Welcome to La Cucaracha!
JONATHAN. Yes, it is nice, isn't it?
GABBY. Hi, I'm 2-C. Can I borrow some Raid?
JONATHAN. I'm sorry, I don't have any.
TED. Aren't you going to the audition today?
GABBY. Yes, I am. I always spray before going to an audition. It's good to know when I come home there'll be someone waiting there who feels worse than me.

JONATHAN. An audition?! Can I go with you?

GABBY. Sure, but let's hurry!

JONATHAN. I've got to get my music. (*Opens suitcase—it is empty!*) It was full when I left Nebraska!

TED. Welcome to New York!

JONATHAN.

AND THOUGH APARTMENTS AREN'T TOO ROOMY
AND THE SKIES ARE ALWAYS GLOOMY . . .

GABBY.

THROUGH MY WINDOW EVERY MORNING I SEE
    GRAY!

TED.

BUT I DON'T HAVE TO SEE AN OCEAN,
AND I DON'T NEED SUNBURN LOTION,

ALL.

CAUSE I ONLY SEE THE SUN AN HOUR A DAY!
WE'D NEVER LEAVE NEW YORK FOR SOME
    SUBURB OUT SOMEWHERE;
I HATED RAKING LEAVES AND I CAN DO
    WITHOUT FRESH AIR!

GABBY.

I LOVE A TAXI RIDE WITH CABS RACING NECK
    AND NECK!

TED.

I DON'T MIND WALKING SIXTY BLOCKS TO
    CASH A CHECK!

GABBY.

I DON'T NEED MY ALARM CLOCK TO WAKE
    ME UP EACH MORN . . .

TED.

THERE'LL ALWAYS BE THE MUSIC OF A
    BLARING HORN!

JONATHAN.

I KNOW I'LL NOT FORGET THE YEARS SPENT
    HERE, BUT STILL . . .

GABBY and TED.

IF YOU'RE VERY, VERY LUCKY, THERE'S A
    CHANCE PERHAPS YOU WILL!

ALL.

BUT IT'S A JOY, JUST A JOY (YOU CAN'T
    IMAGINE)
ADJUSTING TO MANHATTAN LIFE!

(*BLACKOUT.*)

(*Fade up to* JONATHAN *and* GABBY *on the sidewalk. Members of the cast are bustling back and forth simulating bored, hurried, and tense New Yorkers. Music begins.*)

GABBY. Where were you?

JONATHAN. A man asked me for a quarter for a cup of coffee.

GABBY. You didn't give it to him, did you?

JONATHAN. Well, yes . . . but then he wanted a nickel for the tip!!

GABBY. That's silly; you should have told him to go to a takeout counter so he wouldn't have to tip!

JONATHAN. I didn't think of that! (*The bustling New Yorkers have begun to do strange choreographed hand movements surrounding* JONATHAN *and* GABBY. *The song vamp continues.*) Boy, there sure are a lot of strange people on the streets. Why don't they lock them up or something?

GABBY. Lock them up?! (*She leads him over to the side of the stage and joins the other four to sing:*)

CAST. (*Except* JONATHAN.)
WHERE WOULD WE BE WITHOUT PERVERTS?
THEY GIVE THE PAPERS SUCH CHARM!
THEY BRIGHTEN OUR LIVES WITH ADVENTURE
SO HOW COULD WE WISH THEM HARM?

THINK OF A RIDE ON THE SUBWAY
WITHOUT SEVERAL NUTS IN YOUR CAR!
NEW YORK WOULD LOSE ITS DISTINCTION;
THEY'RE THE BEST-BILLED PERFORMERS BY
        FAR!

JENETTE.
THEY'RE IMPETUOUS, INCESTUOUS,
AND SOMETIMES CHILD MOLESTUOUS,
BUT THEY ALWAYS ENTERTAIN WITH WHAT
        THEY DO!
GABBY.
ON THE BUSSES THEY MAKE FUSSES
WHEN THEY TRY TO SHOW THEIR TRUSSES,
        ALL.
BUT YOU KNOW THEY WILL PROVIDE A LAUGH
        OR TWO!
TED. (*Spoken.*) Nice leather we're having!

WHERE WOULD WE BE WITHOUT PERVERTS?
THERE'D BE NO MORE SHOCKS ON TV!
CRIME WOULD LOSE ALL OF ITS VI'LENCE,
AND MOVIES WOULD ALL BE P.G.!

(Chant:)
WHO COULD WRITE A MYSTERY?
AND THINK OF BORING HISTORY
WITH NO MARQUIS DE SADE OR RIPPER JACK!
YOU DON'T HAVE TO PAY ADMISSION TO THEIR
    SIDEWALK EXHIBITION,
    HEATHER.
AND I NEVER MET A NECROPHILIAC I DIDN'T
    LIKE!
    OTHERS.
VO DO DEE OH DOH!
    HEATHER. Everybody sing! (TED *shouts out lyrics like Mitch Miller; first verse is repeated as if it were a sing-a-long.*)

WHERE WOULD WE BE WITHOUT BELOVED
    PERVERTS?
    MEN.
PLEASE LEND AN EAR, V. VAN GOGH.
    WOMEN.
WISH YOU WERE HERE, E. ALLEN POE!
    ALL.
YOUR DEVIATIONS WERE SO CLASSY,
    TED.
THEN THERE'S ME; I JUST LOVE LASSIE!
    ALL.
YOU HAVE HELPED TO SHAPE OUR WORLD;
    WAY TO GO!

(BLACKOUT.)

(Fade up to JONATHAN *and* GABBY *outside Improvisation, reading casting notice in BACKSTAGE.)*

    JONATHAN. *(Reading.)* "I'll Die If I Can't Live Forever revue casting comedy performers, 20-30 who sing and dance . . ."
    GABBY. Is this the Improvisation?
    JONATHAN. That's what it says, but somehow I'd expected something different. You'd better wait here. It doesn't look like a nice place for a woman.

GABBY. It's not so nice out here either; I'll come with you.

JONATHAN. (*Looking around as they enter.*) I guess this is it. Remind me to wash my hands before we leave.

GABBY. It's not so bad. At least it's warm.

JONATHAN. What do we do now?

GABBY. Wait.

JONATHAN. I'm so nervous. I'll die if I don't make it in show business. I've always wanted that. You know, when I was a little kid and everyone else wanted to be a fireman or a farmer, I never wanted any of those things. Used to have this dream when I'd be sitting in the Bijou theater in Omaha and I'd look up at that screen and I'd know what I wanted to be!

GABBY. What?

JONATHAN. Fred Astaire's tap shoes. Not even Fred Astaire. Just his tap shoes. Not even the whole pair. Just one shoe. One single tap.

GABBY. Right or left?

JONATHAN. Right, I think.

GABBY. That's beautiful. Don't give up. Be ready when your chance comes and take it. Keep practicing.

JONATHAN. I practice night and day!

GABBY. I love Cole Porter.

JONATHAN and GABBY. (*They sing:*)
MY LIFE'S A MUSICAL COMEDY
I'M SINGING EVERY DAY;
EACH EVENING'S A PERFORMANCE
AND EACH NOON'S A MATINEE.
THE PLOT IS NEVER BORING FOR THERE'S
    NEVER A REPEAT,
I PLAY A DIFFERENT ROLE FOR EVERY PERSON
    THAT I MEET!
THERE'S ALWAYS LOTS OF LAUGHS, CAUSE,
    BROTHER, YOU SHOULD SEE MY FRIENDS,
AND EVERY DAY I'M WONDERING JUST HOW
    THE STORY ENDS.
    JONATHAN.
I SING ALOUD MY SHOPPING LISTS AND
    TAP AROUND THE STORE
THE BUTCHER AND THE BAKER ALWAYS
    WHISTLE OUT FOR MORE.
I SHUFFLE DOWN THE SIDEWALK AND I YODEL
    IN THE CAR
    JONATHAN and GABBY.
IF SCOUTS WERE IN THE SHOWER THEN BY NOW
    I'D BE A STAR!

GABBY.
I HUM WHEN I AM WRITING AND MY LETTERS
    ALWAYS RHYME
I'VE LEARNED TO TYPE IN RHYTHM; I PREFER
    THREE QUARTER TIME.
THE RADIO'S MY PARTNER AND I LOVE TO USE
    THE PHONE
    JONATHAN and GABBY.
I'VE WORKED OUT SEVERAL CHORUSES THAT
    USE THE BUSY TONE!
    JONATHAN.
YOU SHOULD HEAR THE CLEVER DIALOGUE
    AND INTIMATING FACTS
THAT EACH YEAR I'VE INCLUDED WHEN I
    WRITE MY INCOME TAX.
EXCUSES WHEN I'M LATE ARE ALMOST ALWAYS
    GOOD FOR LAUGHS.
I DON'T MIND SIGNING CHECKS, I JUST
    PRETEND THEY'RE AUTOGRAPHS!
    GABBY.
I LOVE TO WATCH COMMERCIALS AND I ALWAYS
    SING ALONG,
IF YOU TELL ME I AM SHALLOW, I WILL WRITE
    IT IN A SONG.
    JONATHAN and GABBY.
THE STORY OF MY CHILDHOOD IS A SOURCE OF
    ENDLESS SMILES,
AND MY BROKEN-UP ROMANCES KEEP 'EM
    ROLLING IN THE AISLES!

MY LIFE'S A MUSICAL COMEDY I'M SINGING
    EVERY DAY . . . etc. . . .
AND EVERY DAY I'M WONDERING JUST HOW
    THE STORY ENDS.
I HOPE IT'S HAPPY!
JUST HOW THE STORY ENDS!

(*They kiss behind opened umbrellas which were used as
    "canes" for the song . . . very old movie-ish. Fade to
    closing, aperture spot on them, then lights up.*)

JENETTE. (*Entering.*) Hi Gabby!
GABBY. Hi. Jenette Morrison . . . Jonny Winslow.
JENETTE. Hi.
JONATHAN. Hi.

GABBY. This is his first audition.

JENETTE. First audition?

JONATHAN. Yeah.

JENETTE. A virgin, huh?

JONATHAN. (*Meekly.*) That, too. (TED *enters.*) Hi, Ted. (*Attempting a confidence.*) Oh, Ted, this is Jenette Morrison.

TED. Yes, I know. (*They split quickly to opposite sides of stage.*)

JONATHAN. (*To* GABBY.) They must know each other.

GABBY. Only slightly. They're married.

TED. I didn't know you'd be here today. I thought you were working Temp.

JENETTE. I thought you were collecting unemployment, so I took the day off.

TED. Well, what'll we do now? You know we always jinx each other at auditions.

(*Music introduction to "Strangers" comes up. Lights start slow fade to separate spots on the two.*)

JENETTE. I know. Maybe this time it'll work out.

TED. I doubt it.

JENETTE. It never has.

TED. We've never gotten anything together.

JENETTE. Except an apartment. (*Sings:*)

WE'RE STRANGERS WHO SLEEP SIDE BY SIDE;
   (*They stand across the stage from each other in lonely spotlights.*)
SEPARATED BY A WALL OF CHILDISH PRIDE
WE BUILT OURSELVES.
WE'RE STRANGERS WHO SLEEP SIDE BY SIDE.
I NEVER SEEM TO REACH YOU, OUR MOODS
   NEVER MATCHED;
IF I FEEL WARM AND LOVING YOU ARE
   STRANGELY DETACHED.
   TED.
WE'RE STRANGERS WHO SLEEP SIDE BY SIDE:
THE TRUTH IS ONLY SOMETHING SECRET
   THAT WE HIDE
AND WON'T ADMIT.
WE'RE STRANGERS WHO SLEEP SIDE BY SIDE,
OUR QUESTIONS NEVER ANSWERED
OUR PROBLEMS NEVER SHARED.
TO TAKE THE RISK OF TRUSTING IS THE ACT
   WE NEVER DARED.

JENETTE and TED. (*In counterpoint melodies:*)
WE'RE STRANGERS WHO SLEEP SIDE BY SIDE
OUR NEED FOR HAVING ONE ANOTHER WE
    DENIED;
NOW IT'S TOO LATE.
WE'RE STRANGERS WHO SLEEP SIDE BY SIDE;
THE SECURITY OF LOVE IS SOMETHING I HAVE
    NEVER KNOWN,
AND SOMETIME IN THE FUTURE I WILL LEARN
    TO SLEEP ALONE.

TED.
WE'RE STRANGERS WHO SLEEP SIDE BY SIDE.

(HEATHER *enters, greets others then turns,* DAN *enters.*)

DAN. Heather!
HEATHER. Dan! (*They hug.*)
JONATHAN. Married?
GABBY. Roommates. (*He looks shocked.*) Purely platonic. (*He looks confused.*)
JONATHAN. Hi.
DAN. How's it going in there?
GABBY. Slow.
JENETTE. You might as well settle in for a long winter's nap.
DAN. (*To* HEATHER.) Where have you been? I was about to call the police.
HEATHER. Miss me?
DAN. I missed your underwear in the bathroom . . . the scent of drying elastic.
HEATHER. Awwww.
DAN. Where have you been drying your nylons these days?
HEATHER. Oh, Dan, he is so divine! He has a town house on the East Side with four floors and a garden and a terrace and a *huge* Great Dane.
DAN. A whole town house! Is there room for me?
HEATHER. Bringing a roommate to an affair is gauche.
DAN. Well, actually, it's just as well you've been away. I've had company myself. I hope you don't mind . . . I borrowed your nightgown.
HEATHER. (*Raises an eyebrow.*) Which one of you wore it?
DAN. They both did.
HEATHER and DAN. (*They sing:*)
SIN, THAT'S WHAT WE LIVE IN,
BUT WE'D NEVER BEGIN TO SIN
TOGETHER.

(*This is a "beguine"* . . . *they do Tango steps through-out.*)

DAN.
SHE HAS HER SIN IN HER ROOM;
I HAVE MY SIN IN MINE.
OUR RELATIONSHIPS ARE LEGION,
BUT THEY NEVER INTERTWINE.
HEATHER and DAN.
WE'RE ROOMMATES!
WE'LL NEVER BE BRIDE AND GROOMMATES!
OUR AFFAIR TRANSCENDS SALACIOUS LUST
CAUSE WE ARE JUST
VERY GOOD FRIENDS,
WHO LIVE IN . . .
SIN, MUCH TO THE CHAGRIN
OF RELATIONS AND KIN
WHO'VE BEEN
TO SEE US.
HEATHER.
MY DADDY DEAR CAN'T LIVE WITH
MY MODERN WAY OF LIFE,
SO I'VE TOLD HIM IN A FEW YEARS
I WILL BE YOUR COMMON LAW WIFE.
HEATHER and DAN.
WE'RE ROOMMATES!
WE'RE SIMPLY DUSTPAN AND BROOMMATES!
AND BOTH OF US FEEL BY THIS DEAL
OUR LIFE IS ONE LONG TRIP
WHICH REAFFIRMS
IN LEGAL TERMS
OUR LIMITED PARTNERSHIP!

JENETTE. Listen, I've got a funny feeling about this audition.
TED. Why?
JENETTE. I think they're typing first.
JONATHAN. They want typing? I can type!
HEATHER. Good, you'll need it for Office Temps.
JONATHAN. (*Slightly miffed.*) How long have we been waiting?
TED. I don't have a watch.
JENETTE. There must be a calendar around here somewhere.
GABBY. I brought special revue material I wrote. I'd hate to have it go to waste after all that extra work.
JONATHAN. I'd like to see it. Do it for us!

GABBY. Oh, no . . . I'd be too embarrassed.

HEATHER. Well, this may be your only chance to perform it.

GABBY. Well, all right. (*She rushes behind screen Onstage Left,* JONATHAN *follows to help her get into outfit.*)

TED. (*Crosses to* JENETTE.) I think I'd better leave. I'll just spoil your chances.

JENETTE. No, I should go. It's only right. You stay.

TED. No, you stay.

JENETTE. Well, you stay, too.

TED. Only if you stay.

JENETTE. All right. But I'll jinx you.

TED. Don't be silly. (*Pause.*) I didn't want the part anyway.

JENETTE. Then maybe you should go.

JONATHAN. (*They re-enter.*) Quiet everybody! And here she is . . . Miss Gabrielle Schwartz, accompanying herself on the . . .

GABBY. Tape recorder. (*She is wearing a Minnie Pearl hat, carrying a stringless guitar, and has a cassette recorder strung over one shoulder which she punches. It plays a rather complex guitar accompaniment which she tries only halfheartedly to "fake" on her guitar. The tape recorder joins her in harmony in the latter part of the song. She sings the following in a very Country-Western manner: Lights down to half and spot on* GABBY.)

I'M GONNA START AT THE BEGINNING OF
    WHAT YOU DONE TO ME;
JUST LOOK AT THE RESULTZ OF ALL YER
    INFIDELITY!

A IS "AT THE SQUARE DANCE" WHERE YER
    WHITE SOCKS CAUGHT MY EYE.
B IS FER "BELIEF IN YOU." I NEVER THOUGHT
    YOU'D LIE.
O IS FER THE "ORANGE BLOSSOMS" ON OUR
    WEDDIN' DAY
R IS WHUT I SEEN YOU DO; I SEEN YOU "RUN
    AWAY."

T IS FER MY "TINDER HEART" JIST BURSTIN'
    OUT WITH LOVE.
I IS MY "INITIAL" ON YER FAV'RITE BASEBALL
    GLOVE.
O IS "OUR OLD OVEN" WHERE I COOKED FER
    YOU WITH PRIDE.
N IS FER THE "KNOTS" I GOT ALL TANGLED
    UP INSIDE.

A—B—O—R—T—I—O—N WHAT YOU MADE ME DO!
A—B—O—R—T—I—O—N MAKES A PERSON BLUE.
    (*Harmony with recorder here.*)
I'LL ADMIT YOU GAVE ME MONEY AND YOU
    WISHED ME "LOTSA LUCK."
I GOT THE NICEST DOCTOR I COULD FIND FER
    TWENTY BUCK . . . "S."
MY MOMMA SAID THAT MEN WOULD ONLY DO
    ME DIRT!
SHE'S RIGHT BECAUSE EACH TIME I THINK OF
    YOU, I HURT.

(*Lights back up to full.*)

JONATHAN. Gabby, that was great! Better than anything on television.

GABBY. I can't get this off.

JONATHAN. I'll help you. (*He aids her in taking off guitar.*)

HEATHER. The kid learns fast.

GABBY. He's just helping. He's awfully sweet!

JONATHAN. No, I'm not really. I'm a tiger when aroused.

GABBY. Ooo. (*They exit behind screen with country western props.*)

JENETTE. (*Crosses to* TED.) You'll never get in this revue with me here. I'll leave. (*There is no response. She is miffed.*) I said, "I'M LEAVING."

TED. Are you kidding? You can't leave. You'll get the job.

JENETTE. Aw, come on.

TED. No, I mean it. You'll get the job.

JENETTE. Stop that. Now I'll die if I don't get it.

TED. So will I.

JENETTE. A double funeral. Our first shared billing.

HEATHER. I'm hungry. Maybe I could leave and get a sandwich and come back.

(*THE ENTIRE COMPANY SHOUTS FOOD ORDERS SIMULTANEOUSLY IN HUBBUB.*)

HEATHER. (*Turns back and recites.*) Right. (*Crosses to exit.*) That's one egg salad, a rare roast beef on rye, lettuce, mustard, no butter, salt on the side, a sour dill pickle, a BLT on toast, pizza with pepperoni and mushrooms, two coffees, one with milk, one without, a milk, and two Pepsis.

GABBY. You forgot the Twinkies!

HEATHER. AND TWINKIES! (*Stalks off.*)

DAN. And hurry.

JONATHAN. She forgot her pocketbook. (*Indicates* HEATHER's *pocketbook still hanging on the wall.*)

DAN. That isn't where she keeps her money.

JONATHAN. It isn't?

DAN. No, and it's embarrassing. She was once arrested trying to make correct change on a bus.

JONATHAN. I tried hiding money in my shoe, but it gave me terrible blisters . . . Especially the tokens.

HEATHER. Wouldn't you know! I should have gone out sooner. The stage manager says they'll be ready for us in five minutes. Sorry, gang.

JENETTE. That's all right. I shouldn't eat before I sing anyway.

JONATHAN. Me neither. Five minutes!

(*They all sing "TAKE ME" which is piecings of every actors' internal monologue while waiting for an audition combined with typical interactions, jealousies and mistrust of the directors and producers. Five chairlike letters spelling out the word "REVUE" were used in the New York production for all set pieces. They are moved about during this number.*)

ALL.
I SING, I DANCE,
AT A MOMENT'S NOTICE I CAN LAUGH OR CRY!
THEY WILL SOON SEE:
NONE OF MY COMPETITORS ARE HALF
    AS GOOD AS I
COULD BE,
IF THEY'LL JUST TAKE ME, TAKE ME, TAKE ME!
    HEATHER.
MY RESUME DEMONSTRATES HOW FAR BELOW
MY USUAL STANDARDS I'M NOW FORCED TO GO,
BY WAITING TO SING FOR THIS CABARET SHOW.
THE MOMENT THEY SEE ME, I WANT THEM
    TO KNOW:
    ALL.
HOW MANY OTHER THINGS
ARE WAITING IN THE WINGS!
HOW THOSE AGENTS STAND IN LINE,
SIMPLY BEGGING ME TO SIGN!
BUT JUST IN CASE,
I'LL KEEP MY PLACE,

HOPING FOR THAT FAR-FLUNG POSSIBILITY
THAT THEY MIGHT TAKE ME,
SINCE

I SING, I DANCE,
AT A MOMENT'S NOTICE I CAN LAUGH OR CRY!
THEY WILL SOON SEE:
NONE OF MY COMPETITORS ARE HALF AS
    GOOD AS I
COULD BE,
IF THEY'LL JUST TAKE ME, TAKE ME, TAKE ME!
  TED.
I TAPPED RINGS AROUND GENE KELLY IN A
    NINETEEN THIRTIES SPOOF.
  GABBY.
I WAS TZIETEL IN THE MOVIE OF FIDDLER ON
    THE ROOF.
  JENETTE.
JUST LOOK AT ALL THE SINGING LEADS
    THEY'VE LISTED IN MY BIO—MARIAN, ELIZA,
    GUENEVERE . . .
  ALL. (*Spoken.*) Here?
  JENETTE. (*Embarrassed. Spoken.*) No, in Ohio.
  DAN.
I'M SURE THEY'LL HAVE ME READ FOR THE
    MALE ROMANTIC LEAD!
  HEATHER.
I'M CERTAIN I WILL GET FIRST REFUSAL ON
    SOUBRETTE!
  JONATHAN.
LOOK IN THE PAPER, JUST WHO WROTE THIS
    SHOW?
PERHAPS I WON'T STAY IF IT'S NO ONE I KNOW.
  ALL. (*Chanted.*)
WHAT ELSE IS IN THE PAPER?
  HEATHER.
OPEN CALLS FOR "FEELIN' GROOVY."
  TED and JENETTE.
OH GREAT, LET'S GO TO THAT!
  JONATHAN.
NO, IT'S A PORNOGRAPHIC MOVIE.
  GABBY.
LET'S TRY ANOTHER PAPER,
  TED.
"NEEDED: DANCERS . . . STARS AND STRIPES"

DAN and HEATHER.
THAT SOUNDS LIKE JUST THE THING FOR US!
TED and GABBY.
NO, ONLY ETHNIC TYPES!
ALL. (*Sung.*)
I SING, I DANCE, ETC. . . . (*Repeat chorus.*)
DAN.
I'VE GOT THE SAME FEELING I'VE HAD IN THE
    PAST
WHENEVER I READ FOR A SHOW THAT'S BEEN
    CAST.
THAT PERSON WHO'LL SEE US, HE MERELY
    PRETENDS
BECAUSE THE DIRECTOR HAS CAST ALL HER
    FRIENDS!
ALL.
YOU'RE KIDDING! IS THAT TRUE?
I'VE GOT BETTER THINGS TO DO
THAN WAITING IN A CLUMP
FOR A CHANCE TO PLAY THIS DUMP!
WE'D ALL LIKE TO TELL
THOSE PRODUCERS IN THERE
THEY CAN ALL GO TO HELL
CAUSE WE REALLY DON'T CARE . . .
STAGE MANAGER. (*Shouted. Offstage.*) Next!
ALL. (*Weakly.*)
. . . ALL THAT MUCH.
BUT JUST IN CASE
I'LL KEEP MY PLACE
HOPING FOR THAT LOVELY POSSIBILITY THAT
    THEY JUST MIGHT . . .

(JONATHAN *does obligato here.*)

TAKE ME, TAKE ME, TAKE ME, TAKE ME,
    TAKE ME,
TAKE ME, TAKE ME, TAKE ME, TAKE ME,
    TAKE ME,
I'M A SPARKLING PERSONALITY
OBSERVE MY GENIALTY
I OOZE WITH SEXUALITY AND
TALK SHOW INFORMALITY
AND SUPERFICIALITY
I REEK THEATRICALITY . . .
TAKE ME, TAKE ME, TAKE ME, ME ME TAKE
    ME TAKE ME!

DAN. Well, I don't know about anybody else, but I'm going in.

HEATHER. Let me check first. (*Exits.*)

TED. They must not have any budget. They should have somebody out here running the audition, a sign-in sheet, or something.

JENETTE. They could at least show some respect for the actors.

DAN. I'd settle for less respect and more work.

HEATHER. Okay, we can go in now. (*Noisy ad libbing, all exit except* JONATHAN.) Jonathan, the stage manager said they just spent an hour auditioning the juveniles from PIPPIN and CANDIDE. I think your part is probably cast.

JONATHAN. Well, what should I do? I've waited this long.

HEATHER. Why waste your time? You don't have any pull.

JONATHAN. Doesn't talent mean anything?

HEATHER. If it did, I'd be working.

JONATHAN. Well, it can't hurt to try.

HEATHER. Go ahead if you want to. Just don't be too disappointed.

JONATHAN. You mean, I haven't got a chance?

HEATHER. I wish I could say you did. You understand, don't you?

JONATHAN. Yeah . . . I guess so . . . thanks. (*Lights fade to follow spot on* JONATHAN. *He chants:*)

YOU CAN ALWAYS FIND A PERSON WHO WILL
    SAY YOU CAN'T,
THAT YOU MUSTN'T EVEN TRY.
"GIVE IT UP AT ONCE," THEY'LL SAY AND LIST
    THE REASONS WHY.
THEY'LL TELL YOU OF A FRIEND THEY HAD
    WHO MADE THE SAME MISTAKE
OF HOPING HE WOULD BE THE ONE TO GET
    THE EVEN BREAK.
HE DIDN'T LOOK AT NUMBERS, DIDN'T COUNT
    THE COMPETITION.
    (*Sung:*)
"THE FOOL . . . HE NEVER LOOKED BEYOND HIS
    OWN AMBITION."

THERE'S ALWAYS SOMEONE WHO'LL TELL YOU
    "NO."
WHO'LL SAY "DON'T DO IT" AND CAN'T WAIT
    TO SAY "I TOLD YOU SO!"

THERE'S ALWAYS SOMEONE WHO'LL SAY "JUST
    FORGET IT"
"YOU THINK THE MOMENT MAY SLIP BY?
    SOMETIMES IT'S BEST TO LET IT!"
"YOU'RE TOO YOUNG." "YOU'RE TOO OLD." "IT'S
    NOW TOO LATE."
"YOU SHOULD HAVE STARTED SOONER." "NO,
    IT'S BEST TO WAIT."
"DO YOU KNOW WHAT THE ODDS ARE, AT
    LEAST BE AWARE . . .
"THINGS ARE WORSE NOW THAN EVER, YOU
    HAVEN'T GOT A PRAYER!"

THERE'S ALWAYS SOMEONE WHO'LL TELL YOU
    "NO"
IF YOU LET THEM,
IF YOU LISTEN.
THEY ARE ALWAYS THERE,
BUT I HAVEN'T LISTENED YET AND I REFUSE
    TO CARE.
IT MAY BE IMPROBABLE I'LL FIND SUCCESS
BUT YOU'LL HEAR ME SAY ANYTHING BUT
    "YES!"
THERE'S ALWAYS SOMEONE WHO'LL TELL
    YOU "NO,"
BUT I REFUSE TO HEAR.
I REFUSE TO HEAR!

(BLACKOUT.)

(*Enter* DAN, GABBY, HEATHER *congratulating each other.
    Lights up to full.*)

    GABBY. I can't believe it! They laughed all the way through
my song!
    HEATHER. But we got it!
    TED. (*Rushing in.*) We did it!
    JENETTE. (*Just behind him.*) Our first show together!
    TED. It's wonderful.
    JENETTE. Maybe we're good luck for each other after all.
(*They kiss.*)
    TED. Great!
    JENETTE and TED. I hope we don't have any numbers to-
gether!

(*All are putting on their distinctive coats and hats, in order to be dressed by start of "Oh Boy."*)

JONATHAN. (*Entering.*) Gabby, Gabby, Gabby, I got it, I got it. I went in there and sang and they said, I forget, and then I did some steps for them and then, I forget, and they said I got the part and to come to the rehearsal on . . . I forget. I'll have to go back in and find out . . .

GABBY. On Monday.

JONATHAN. That's right. On Monday! How did you guess!

GABBY. I'm telegraphic.

HEATHER. I got it, too. We all did! (*Music under starts.*)

JONATHAN. You did? Everybody did? Oh boy! Wait'll I tell Mom!

ALL. (*Sing fugue:*)

OH BOY, OH BOY, OHHHHHHHBOY, OH BOY, OH BOY, OH BOY, OH BOY, ETC. . . . JUST WAIT'LL I TELL MOM, OH BOY, OH BOY!

(*BLACKOUT.*)

(*Exeunt all but* JONATHAN. *All are in darkness in wings except* JONATHAN *who is in dim light rehearsing on stage with pianist. He is again in rehearsal clothes.*)

JONATHAN. We're actors, and there're people who think we must take drugs and drink and we meet for . . .

HEATHER. (*Shouts from wings.*) I CAN'T FIND MY TAP SHOES!

DAN. (*Shouts.*) THEY'RE ON MY CHAIR!

HEATHER. SORRY.

JONATHAN. We're actors, and there're people who think . . .

TED. (*Shouts.*) WHERE ARE MY PROPS?

JENETTE. (*Shouts.*) I PUT THEM IN THE PROP CLOSET WHERE THEY BELONG.

TED. (*Shouts.*) THAT'S AFTER THE SHOW, NOT DURING!

JENETTE. (*Shouts.*) HERE! (*Loud crash.*)

TED. OW! JENETTE.

JONATHAN. We're actors, and there're people who think we must take drugs. . . .

GABBY. (*Shouts.*) THAT WAS THE LONGEST DRESS REHEARSAL I'VE EVER BEEN THROUGH.

JONATHAN. PLEASE BE QUIET!

GABBY. (*Entering.*) I'm sorry. I didn't realize you were still rehearsing.

JONATHAN. We open in twenty-four hours and they just sprang this solo on me. I'll never remember it.

GABBY. You'll remember it. And they'll remember you. Twenty-four hours! Oi!

JONATHAN. (*Musingly.*) Twenty-four hours . . . (*Lights very gradually fade up so they are up full by the time others enter.* JONATHAN *sings:*)

TWENTY FOUR HOURS FROM THIS MOMENT
    WE HAVE TO OPEN A SHOW.
TWENTY FOUR HOURS, TWENTY FOUR HOURS,
    THAT'S NOT LONG TO GO!
TWENTY FOUR HOURS FROM THIS MOMENT I'LL
    BE ALONE IN THE LIGHT.
TWENTY FOUR HOURS, TWENTY FOUR HOURS,
    IS THIS EXCITEMENT OR FRIGHT?
THERE'LL BE NO ONE ELSE BESIDE ME WHEN
    IT'S TIME TO SING MY SONG.
THEY'LL ALL BE LOOKING STRAIGHT AT ME;
WILL I GET THE WORDS ALL WRONG?

THERE'LL BE NOTHING TO HIDE ME BUT
    MAKE UP,
IF THEY BREAK UP
WITH LAUGHTER,
AND AFTER
IT'S OVER, WHAT THEN?
    (*All others enter in rehearsal clothes carrying tap shoes and put them on as they sing.*)
TWENTY FOUR HOURS FROM THIS MOMENT
    WE HAVE TO OPEN A SHOW.
TWENTY FOUR HOURS, TWENTY FOUR HOURS,
    THAT'S NOT LONG TO GO.
SOON AS I'M SAFELY IN MY COSTUME, READY
    TO GO AND ON TIME,
YESTERDAY'S WORRIES SEEM FORGOTTEN, BUT
    TILL THAT'S HAPPENING I'M

BESET WITH ONE FEAR: WILL THEY LIKE US?
WILL THEY STRIKE US
AS FRIENDLY,
BUT THEN LEAVE
BEFORE WE ARE THROUGH.

(*Chant:*)
TWENTY FOUR HOURS FROM THIS MOMENT WE
    HAVE TO OPEN A SHOW.
TWENTY FOUR HOURS, TWENTY FOUR HOURS,
    THAT'S NOT LONG TO GO!
    (*They tap out rhythm.*)
AT THE END OF TWENTY FOUR HOURS
WILL WE GET CLOSED DOWN OR FLOWERS?
    (*They tap out rhythm. Tap break.*)
    (*Sung:*)
TWENTY FOUR HOURS FROM THIS MOMENT WE
    HAVE TO OPEN A SHOW!
TWENTY FOUR HOURS, TWENTY FOUR HOURS,
    THAT'S NOT LONG TO GO!
TWENTY FOUR HOURS FROM THIS MOMENT WE
    HAVE TO OPEN A SHOW
AT NINTH AVENUE AND FORTY-FOURTH STREET,
FORTY-FOURTH STREET AND NINTH A-VE-NUE
    (*Tap*)!

END OF ACT ONE

(*Actors recess, singing: Lights fade to house lights.*)

ALL.
IT'S INTERMISSION, IT'S INTERMISSION, PLEASE
    DON'T GO HOME,
IT'S JUST INTERMISSION;
AND THEN WE'LL CALL YOU IN,
AGAIN WE WILL BEGIN,
BUT JUST FOR NOW,
IT'S INTERMISSION.

INTERMISSION

ACT TWO

All actors have on evening dress from now on.

The Pianist plays an entr'acte which uses the opening number and begins the Improvisation song. The lights fade up as the same three singers of the First Act Improvisation song are crossing back onto the stage in the same step they used earlier to cross off.

HEATHER, JENETTE, and DAN. (*They are mouthing the following words:*)
LEGENDS STILL HAVE IT THAT EVEN DICK
 CAVETT
FELL ON HIS FACE IN THIS VERY SAME PLACE.
 (*Lights are now up to full. They sing:*)
LET'S HEAR IT FOR THE TACKY, KINKY, FUNKY,
 FADED
HOLE-IN-THE-WALL AND JUNKY JADED
IMPROVISATION!!

HERE WE ARE AT THE IMPROV, THE
 IMPROVISATION!
WE'RE ABOUT TO PRESENT JUST ONE MORE
 MUSICAL REVUE.
 HEATHER.
IT ISN'T THE UPSTAIRS,
 JENETTE.
OR EVEN THE DOWNSTAIRS.
 DAN.
WE CAN'T TAKE OFF OUR CLOTHES HERE,
 ALL.
BUT I GUESS IT'LL HAVE TO DO.

WE CAN'T REPRISE THIS SONG AGAIN
BUDD FRIEDMAN WANTS US THROUGH BY TEN.
 GIRLS.
MAYBE YOUR GLASS HAS A FAINT LIPSTICK
 RING,
 ALL.
BUT EVEN YOUR WAITRESS ACT, DANCE AND
 SING . . .

(*Other three enter and join in.*)

AT NINTH AVENUE AND FORTY-FOURTH
    STREET!
    MEN.
STILLER, MEARA, FREDDY PRINZE, AND COMIC
    DAVID FRYE
DODGED THE MUGGERS ON THIS BLOCK,
    JONATHAN.
AND, NOW, SO CAN I!
    GIRLS.
WHEN SHE WAS IN FIDDLER,
UNDAUNTED MISS MIDDLER
TRIED OUT HER SONGS
ON THESE ELEGANT THRONGS!
    ALL.
LET'S HEAR IT FOR THE TACKY, KINKY, FUNKY,
    FADED
HOLE-IN-THE-WALL AND JUNKY JADED
IMPROVISATION.

(*BLACKOUT. Much whispering . . . getting into places. Pin
    spot comes up on* TED *Center Stage, very much the
    "Evangelist."*)

    TED. (*Chanted.*)
HAVE YOU GIVEN THANKS, GIVEN THANKS
    TODAY?
NO, MY FRIENDS, YOU'VE GONE ASTRAY.
WHO GIVES LIGHT AND LIFE TO YOU?
GIVE DEVOTION WHERE IT'S DUE!
WHAT IS THE CONTROLLING FORCE OF ALL
    PURSUITS OF PROFESSIONAL LIFE AND
    DOMESTICITY?
    ALL. (*Spoken.*)
WHAT?
    TED.
WHAT ARE YOU DEPENDENT UPON ABOVE ALL
    ELSE AND CANNOT DO WITHOUT?
    ALL.
WHAT?

            (*All in very choir-like poses.*)
    TED. (*Sung.*)
ELECTRICITY!

(*Lights up to full.*)

ALL.
AMP! WATT!
TED.
ELECTRICAL CURRENT GIVES YOU MEANING,
DOES YOUR HOUSEHOLD CHORES AND
    CLEANING,
TYPES YOUR LETTERS, OPENS CANS,
SHOWS YOU MOVIES, HEATS YOUR PANS,
BLENDS YOUR COCKTAILS, TURNS YOUR FANS!
ALL.
HOSANNA, HOSANNA, AMP! WATT!
TED. (*Chanted.*)
THINK, MY FRIENDS, OF A HOT JULY,
MERCURY IS CLIMBING HIGH!
WADING THROUGH THE HUMID MIRE,
YOU ARE DOOMED TO FEEL THE FIRE!
SATAN SEARS ACROSS YOUR BROW.
WHO COMES TO YOUR RESCUE NOW?
DAN. (*Spoken.*) Who?
TED. (*Sung.*)
ELECTRICAL CURRENT BRINGS SALVATION
WITH EACH VOLT OF CIRCULATION,
FREES YOU FROM YOUR FORCED SUBMISSION
AS IT STARTS TO AIR CONDITION!
ALL.
COOLING, COOLING, COOLING, ALLELUJAH!
TED.
WHO'S THE GOD WE CAN AGREE ON?
ALL.
AGREE ON?
TED.
YOU, ALMIGHTY STEEL AND FREON!
ALL.
AND FREON!
TED.
YOU COME TO US IN OUR HOUR OF NEED,
YOU'RE THE ECUMENICAL CREED!
HEATHER. (*In church soprano voice, taking Madonna pose.
Others form Sistine Chapel picture around her.* TED *is "God"
behind her. Lights fade to atmospheric special on* HEATHER.)
LEAD US BESIDE SOAPY WATERS
AND BANISH ALL REGRET.
KEEP MY CUP RUNNING OVER

BUT DON'T LET MY CORD GET WET!

TED. (*Touching each one à la faith healer. Lights up.*)

ELECTRICAL CURRENT GIVES YOU POWER,
TELLS YOU NEWS AND MARKS EACH HOUR,
RUNS THE SUBWAY,
BRUSHES HAIR,
PLAYS YOU MUSIC, FILTERS AIR,
MAKES YOUR COFFEE, ROCKS YOUR CHAIR!

BOYS.

ELECTRICAL CURRENT ENDS DEPENDENCE ON
     YOUR PEERS AND YOUR
DESCENDANTS.
WITH AN OUTLET AND A PHONE
YOU CAN NEVER BE ALONE!

ALL.

ELECTRICAL CURRENT HEALS FRUSTRATION,
YIELD TO WARMTH AND STIMULATION!
REVEL IN A NEW SENSATION!
IF YOU'RE IN THE MOOD: *VIBRATION!*

BOYS.

BZZZ BZZZ BZZZ BZZZ
IT'S THE BUZZ, IT'S WHATSA HAPPENING

GIRLS. (*Boys continue.*)

VIBRATORS, VIBRATORS!
AMP . . .

DAN, JENETTE, and HEATHER.

WATT A FRIEND WE HAVE IN CURRENT.
IT WILL ALWAYS TURN US ON!

(HEATHER *does obligato here.*)

ALL.

ELECTRICAL CURRENT KEEPS ME LIVING,
HEAR MY PRAISES OF THANKSGIVING!
POP MY POPCORN, TOAST MY BREAD,
ADD MY TAXES, HEAT MY BED!

MEN.

TRIM MY WHISKERS, POACH MY EGGS,

GIRLS.

CLEAN MY CARPETS, SHAVE MY LEGS!

ALL.

YOU WOULD THWART US IF YOU SHORT US!
ALL GLORY LAUD AND HONOR TO THEE,
     TO THEE, TO THEE:

ELECTRICITY!
AMP! WATT!

*(Special effect of lights flashing on and off. BLACKOUT.
    Lights come partially up to dim "Backstage" lighting.)*

GABBY. *(Meeting* JONATHAN *in "Wing" area.)* You're doing
great Jonny!
    DAN. *(Bumping into them. Stage whisper.)* SCUSE ME.
    JONATHAN. Do you really think so?
    GABBY. I know so!
    JONATHAN. I had a dream last night, about the new
solo. . . .
    TED. *(Rushing to them.)* Jonathan . . . I . . . oh! Never
mind. *(He exits.)*
    GABBY. Don't worry about it . . . everyone does that. It's
a good sign if you dream about forgetting your lines!
    JONATHAN. I dreamed I remembered them!

(BLACKOUT . . . lights up . . . spot on HEATHER *at piano
    with red feather boa.)*

    HEATHER.
I NEVER THOUGHT IT WOULD HAPPEN TO
    ME . . .

BUT I'M IN LOVE WITH WALTER CRONKITE,
    WALTER CRONKITE, WALTER CRONKITE.
MY EXULTATION YOU MUST EXCUSE;
IT'S ALMOST TIME FOR THE EVENING NEWS.
YES, I'M IN LOVE WITH WALTER CRONKITE;
THIS SPECIAL SECRET I MUST CONFESS.
WALTER CRONKITE IS MY TRUE LOVE,
AND I'M FAITHFUL TO CBS.

IF I WANT TO SEE THE WORLD, HE CAN TAKE
    ME ANYWHERE.
ALL HIS THOUGHTS TO ME HE MENTIONS
ON POLITICAL CONVENTIONS,
AND THROUGH ALL THE YEARS OF HISTORY,
    WITH WALTER, YOU ARE THERE!

FOR I'M IN LOVE WITH WALTER CRONKITE,
    WALTER CRONKITE, WALTER CRONKITE.
MY HEART BEATS FASTER, MY SENSES ROCK

WHEN IT APPROACHES SEVEN O' CLOCK.
YES, I'M IN LOVE WITH WALTER CRONKITE;
HE IS MY HERO
EACH FIRE AND FLOOD.
I WOULD NEVER, EVER LEAVE HIM . . .
EXCEPT, PERHAPS, FOR ROGER MUDD.

(*BLACKOUT. Whispering, shuffling, arranging "letter-chairs" to sit on.*)

GABBY. (*These lines are all in stage whispers.*) DAN!
DAN. What?
GABBY. You've got my "V!"
DAN. What?
GABBY. You've got my "V." I always sit on "V."
DAN. Well, you can have my "E."
GABBY. I can't sit on an "E"— I'm not shaped that way!
DAN. All right, here. (*Lights come up on the two perfectly poised on the correct letters.*)
DAN.
I'M SO BORED WITH MEDIOCRITY,
SELF-SATISFIED HYPOCRISY,
WITH HEARING THE INGREDIENTS
OF SOAPS AND ANTIPERSPIRANTS.
THAT COCKTAIL PARTY CHATTER TELLS ME
    NOTHING THAT WILL MATTER.
I DON'T WANT TO KNOW THE GOSSIP OF THE
    TOWN!
I HOPE SOMEONE ERASES ALL THOSE LITTLE
    SMILING FACES
AND THOSE DRAWINGS OF THAT DOG WITH
    CHARLIE BROWN!
    (*Spoken.*)
(Which are everywhere!)
ALL. (*Sung.*)
HE HOPES SOMEONE ERASES ALL THOSE LITTLE
    SMILING FACES
AND THOSE DRAWINGS OF THAT DOG WITH
    CHARLIE BROWN.
GABBY.
I'M SO BORED WITH THESE ASTROLOGISTS
AND AMATEUR PSYCHOLOGISTS
WHO WANT TO KNOW WHEN I WAS BORN,
SO THEY CAN GIVE ADVICE AND WARN.

SPEAK NOT OF INFLATION OR THE YOUNGER
    GENERATION,
AND PLEASE DON'T TRY TO ANALYZE MY
    DREAM!
I'LL KEEP RIGHT ON PRAYING THAT ALL
    MUZAK WILL STOP PLAYING,
AND THE SONGS THEY CALL "TOP FORTY"
    MAKE ME SCREAM! AHH!

ALL.
AND SHE'LL KEEP RIGHT ON PRAYING THAT
    ALL MUZAK WILL STOP PLAYING,
AND THE SONGS THEY CALL "TOP FORTY"
    MAKE HER SCREAM! AHHH!

TED.
WHY MUST ALL SALES CLERKS BE RUDE?

ALL.
HO HUM.

HEATHER.
AND MOVIE STARS ALWAYS BE NUDE?

ALL.
HO HUM.

JENETTE.
I OBSERVE CAPITULATION
OF THE WORLD'S IMAGINATION
ALL WIT AND ERUDITION ARE SUBDUED.

ALL. (*Chant:*)
PLEASE TELL ME NO MORE ABOUT RIOTS.
RONALD McDONALD OR DIETS.
I'M TERRIBLY TIRED OF TAXES.
I'M WEARY OF WHITENERS AND WAXES,
AND PEOPLE WITH NOTHING TO SAY:
STEVE LAWRENCE AND EYDIE GORME,
AND SOAP OPERA VERSIONS OF PASSION,
INSIPID OBEYERS OF FASHION,
THE CALORIE COUNT OF A CARROT,
GOD HELP ME IGNORE RONA BARRETT!

(*They line up in a Greek dance formation. All sing:*)

I'M SO BORED WITH POMPOUS PIETY,
THE TALES OF HIGH SOCIETY,
WITH CEREAL THAT POPS AND SNAPS,
AND JOKES ON GENERATION GAPS.

GIRLS.
YOU'LL FIND ME GROWING SURLY

IF YOU QUOTE MISS HELEN GURLY (BROWN),
  Boys.
AND PARDON IF I'M CRABBY AT THE MENTION
    OF DEAR ABBY,
  All.
BUT I HOPE WITH SOME ASSURANCE YOU'LL
    AGREE . . .
UNLESS WE FIND PROTECTION
FROM THIS TEDIOUS INFECTION
SOON WE ALL WILL BE ENVELOPED BY ENNUI!
    (*Chanted.*)
(DON'T DISTURB THE BOURGEOISIE
JOHNNY MANN IS ON TV!)
    (*Sung.*)
WE ALL WILL BE ENVELOPED BY ENNUI,
  Jonathan.
(AND READERS DIGEST!)
  All.
WE ALL WILL BE ENVELOPED BY ENNUI
  Heather and Jenette.
(AND ROD McKUEN!)
  All.
WE ALL WILL BE ENVELOPED BY ENNUI

YAWN.

(*FADE TO BLACK.*)

(Ted *and* Jenette *sit on two of the letters.*)

  Ted.
REMEMBER WHEN A BOY,
TO EARN WHAT HE'D ENJOY,
WOULD HAVE TO WAIT A WEEK
HIS VERY FIRST WORDS TO SPEAK?
HE'D HAVE TO KEEP HIS ARDOR
COOLING IN THE PARLOR,
WAITING FOR THE MOMENT TO BE RIGHT!
HIS REWARD FOR A YEAR WAS THIS:
A VERY VIRGINAL KISS
AND NOTHING ELSE UNTIL THAT WEDDING
    NIGHT!
BUT IN THESE MODERN DAYS
LOVE HAS REACHED A PHASE,

WHERE THE KEY TO HARMONY
IS FOUND IN JUST ONE PHRASE:

MY PLACE OR YOURS?
THE WORDS ONE NEVER IGNORES!
THE SWEETEST INVITATION
IS TO AN ASSIGNATION.
MY PLACE OR YOURS?
THE WORDS ONE JUST ADORES
TODAY.
OUR ATTITUDE'S REALISTIC:
IT'S HARDLY EUPHEMISTIC TO SAY,
"MY PLACE OR YOURS?"
    JENETTE.
YES, NOW, MY DEAR, WE'RE FREE,
WITH TRUE CONVENIENCY.
AT LAST WE'RE WISE
AND RECOGNIZE:
THERE'S MORE FOR TWO THAN TEA!

MY PLACE OR YOURS
    TED.
FOR TWOS FOR THREES OR FOR FOURS!
    JENETTE and TED.
MISGIVINGS WE'VE NOT ANY
    JENETTE.
THERE'S NO SUCH THING AS ONE TOO MANY!
    JENETTE and TED.
MY PLACE OR YOURS.
WHY LATELY WE'VE INVITED SCORES!
    JENETTE.
YOU'RE MY ONE AND ONLY
    TED.
BUT I NEVER WILL BE LONELY
    JENETTE and TED.
AT MY PLACE OR YOURS.
    (*They do a "NO NO NANETTE" soft shoe dance here
    and dance out to:*)
MY PLACE OR YOURS?

(*BLACKOUT.*)

(*Spot up on* HEATHER *and* DAN *in "Wing" area.*)

HEATHER. Well, Ted and Jenette finally seem to be getting
along.

DAN. The jinx is off.

HEATHER. And Gabby and Jonny are doin' pretty well.

DAN. Yep. (*They look at each other.*) My place or yours?

HEATHER. Halfway between and your choice of weapons!

(*BLACKOUT. DAN rushes over to join two other men. Lights up fast.*)

MEN.
WHO GETS ALL THE THANKS
FOR OUR EMPTY SAVINGS BANKS?
WHO HAS EARNED OUR GRATITUDE
FOR EXPENSIVE FUEL AND FOOD,
FOR THE LOSS OF ALL OUR TRUST
IN THE MEN WHO GOVERN US,
WHO WE'D LIKE TO TAKE TO TASK?
DO WE REALLY HAVE TO ASK?

TED.
THANKS, MISTER FORD!
DAN.
THANK YOU, ROCKY!
JONNY.
YES, AND THANK YOU, JOHNNY DEAN.
ALL.
AND ALSO SPIRO
THOUGH YOUR CAREER-O
NOW IS LOOKING PRETTY LEAN.
    (GIRLS *enter and join in here.*)
OUR HEARTS ARE FILLED WITH AMNESTY FOR
    EVERYTHING THEY'VE DONE!
WE'VE GOT A LIST AND WE INSIST ON
    THANKING EVERY ONE!

(*All produce paper rolls with Congress names.*)

DAN. LADIES AND GENTLEMEN. THE 535 ORIG-
INAL MEMBERS OF THE HISTORIC 93rd CONGRESS
OF THE UNITED STATES OF AMERICA! (*Unroll paper rolls.*)

ALL.
SAXBE BAKER KENNEDY O'NEILL
MITCHELL ABZUG HUMPHREY BUCKLEY STEELE
PERCY JAVITS MUSKIE ERVIN BRAY
ANDREWS JACKSON HANRAHAN McKAY!

BELLMOND THURMOND CORMAN BROTZMAN
    ESHLEMAN DERWINSKI
EASTLAND BERGLAND MADIGAN MONTGOMERY
    KLUCZYNSKI
HATHAWAY DOMENICI McCOLLISTER
    HELSTOWSKI
SULLIVAN McCLELLAN MOORHEAD WYLIE
    ROSTENKOWSKI!
    GIRLS.
AIKEN LEHMAN CLANCEY WHELAN REILSBACK
    HALSEY TAYLOR
LATTA ASHLEY VANIK HASTINGS ALBERT
    JARMAN SAYLOR
SANDMAN BARRET MARTIN ASHBROOK
    PARKWOOD CARNEY STRATTON
NATCHA STANTON ABDNOR STAGGERS PARRIS
    HANNA PATTEN!

    BOYS. (*Simultaneously with above.*)
GRIFFIN WILLIAMS WIGGINS HINSHAW NIX
GIBBONS BRINKLEY FINDLEY SHIPLEY HICKS
FISHER MILLER GRIFFITHS BINGHAM WHITE
MILFORD GILMAN CHISHLOM SYMMS
    FULBRIGHT!

    HEATHER.
JOHNSTON COTTON COCHRAN THOMPSON
    JENETTE and GABBY.
FONG!
    JENETTE.
HOLTZMAN PROXMIRE
    DAN.
HORTON MORGAN LONG, THORNTON
    JONATHAN.
MOSS McDONALD DUPONT KOCH
    TED.
ROBERTS JORDAN DOWNING
    TED and JENETTE.
KING
    DAN and GABBY.
FISH
    JONATHAN and HEATHER.
ROE!
    HEATHER.
FULTON BULTER GOODLING ULLMAN PIKE

STUCKEY CULVER RUNNELS DULSKI SIKES
ROONEY SHUSTER GUBSER GUNTER PELL
RYAN EVINS HUDNUT BIBLE BELL!
JONATHAN. (*Simultaneously with above.*)
DONAHUE MAGNUSON BURLESON DEVINE MINK
    PICKLE
SCHNEEBELI McCLORY PINGELL MINCHALL
    QUILLEN NICHOLS
HEMPELMAN MEZVINSKY WYATT MINISH HILLIS
    WITTEN
WAGGONER MATHIAS KYROS SHRIVER BYRON
    LITTON!
JENETTE and GABBY. (*Starts after above verses have begun.*)
RANDALL METCALF CURTIS BENNET PEPPER
    MURPHY STENNIS
HECKLER NELSEN PERKINS MELCHNER BURTON
    EVANS DENNIS
DUNCAN GURNEY BURDICK BENTSEN EDWARDS
    LEGGETT FANNIN
FRENZEL SPARKMAN NUNGATE DELLUMS
    NEDZI HERBERT CANNON
DAN and TED. (*Simultaneously with above.*)
HOLLINGS SCHROEDER CONLAN CRONIN FORD
HOGAN CONYERS FOLEY BROWN ICHORD
OWENS FROELICH BOLAND GROVER COOK
HOSMER CLAUSEN CONTE PROUTY BROOKE!

(*Canon—each of the six singers has two verses.*)

HEATHER.
MARTIN BLATNIK TALCOT HARVEY CLAY
DENHOLM PEARSON STEVENS BYRD OBEY
STEELMAN CLEVELAND KEATING RIEGLE
    TREEN
LANDGREBE TIERNAN BIESTER WILSON GREEN!

BRECKENRIDGE McCLOSKEY FREYLINGHUSEN
    FOUNTAIN COHEN
DOMINICK KUYKENDALL ROSENTHAL
    McCORMACK BOWEN
MALLARY ANNUNZIO INOUYE YATRON PEYSER
SEIBERLING DELANEY McINTYRE ADAMS
    FRASER!

JONATHAN.
ARMSTRONG GAYDOS PREYER MONDALE GINN
WIDNALL STEIGER RANGEL WHITEHURST WINN

ROGERS COTTER JOHNSON COLLINS LOTT
ROYBAL BROYHILL COUGHLIN FORSYTHE SCOTT

HAMMERSCHMIDT RONCALLO MOLLOHAN
    RINALDO TOWELL
CHAMBERLAIN O'HARA DELLENBACK ADDABBO
    POWELL

CONABLE GIAIMO ABOUREZK ZABLOCKI TOWER
BURGENER GOLDWATER CEDERBERG McKINNEY
    FLOWERS
    JENETTE.
PATMAN GRASSO HARSHA WAMPLER MAYNE
FASCELL ARENDS LANDRUM CARNEY CRANE
DAVIS BRASCO HANSEN CAMP McFALL
CARTER PASSMAN RARICK TAFT UDALL!

SARBANE McEWEN HUBER GUDE YOUNG BURKE
    VEYSEY
REGULAR McCLURE GERMAIN ROUSSELOT
    BROCK CASEY
MARAZITI BIGORITO TEAGUE McFADE KEMP
    GETTYS
ROBISON MAZZOLI SPENCE VAN DEERLIN ESCH
    BEARD PETTIS!

    TED.
HRUSKA DULSKI GUYERS HELMS CHAPPELL
BYRD RUSH WOLFF HUNT BROWN BEARD
    BOGGS MICHEL
BROOKS ROTH MOAKLEY ROTH RUTH HUGHES
    PODELL
MOSHER STOKES HOLT BOLLING WARE MIZELL!

MYERS MANN BUCHANAN ALEXANDER WALSH
    OBRIEN
BUFALIS BONZALES DE LA GARZA SNYDER ZION
KAZEN MATSUNAGA KASTENMEIER HAYS
    McSPADDEN
SARASIN SEBLIUS RONCALIO HART MADDEN!

    GABBY.
ASPIN ARCHER GRAVEL HASKELL STARK
TALMADGE HARTKE DANIELS ALLEN CLARK
TUNNEY BARTLETT CRANSTON BOACKBURN
    FREY

WALDIE HAWKINS MATHIS RANDOLPH GREY!

MEEDS AND EDWARDS QUIE RODINO SCHERLE
    SKUBITZ REID
CHURCH NUNN BEGICH HEINZ PRICE KETCHUM
    FUQUA REUSS RUDD STEED
SLACK McGOVERN JAGS ZWACH LUJAN MILLS
    PASTORE DORN
WEICKER WRIGHT STUDDS SISK BADILLO
    BEVILL ERLENBORN!
    DAN.
DOLE MONTOYA MOHON ROY RHODES DENT
FLOOD DIGGS MAILLIARD WYDLER POAGE LENT
SCHWEIKER FLYNT SMITH CHILES BAYH BIDEN
    GROSS
YATES THONE WYMAN JONES KARTH ELIBERG
    ROSE

STEVENSON AND ROBINSON AND SYMINGTON
    AND EAGLETON
AND DICKINSON AND HENDERSON AND
    DANIELSON AND HARRINGTON
AND HUDDLESTON AND ANDERSON AND
    HUTCHINSON AND HAMILTON
MANSFIELD, HATFIELD, BROMFIELD, HOLLI-
    FIELD, STUBBLEFIELD, SATTERFIELD McGEE!

    ALL.
HUMMMMM

(*BLACKOUT. Onstage before lights have come up for next
    number.*)

JENETTE. Oh, Ted, you're doing awfully well.
TED. Nothing like you.
JENETTE. Oh, come on, you're great!
TED. You're the one they really like.
JENETTE. No, you!
TED. Believe me, you're much better than I am.
JENETTE. Ted, you know what I love about you!
TED. What?
JENETTE. You're always right!

(*Lights up.* TED *and* JENETTE *with* HEATHER *and* JONATHAN
    sing:)

ALL.

LET'S HAVE A RODGERS AND HAMMERSTEIN
    AFFAIR:
WE'LL SPEND EACH BEAUTIFUL MORNING HERE
    IN BALI H'AI;

TED and JONATHAN.

ENCHANTED EVENINGS WE'LL HEAR THE SOUND
    OF MUSIC.

HEATHER and JENETTE.

AND DANCE LIKE THE KING AND I!

MEN.

WE'LL WHISTLE WHERE THE WIND SWEEPS
    DOWN THE PLAIN.

WOMEN.

YOUNGER THAN SEVENTEEN OR SPRINGTIME
    I'LL BECOME,

ALL.

AS WE CLIMB EVERY MOUNTAIN

HEATHER.

IN SEARCH OF EDELWEISS
TO DECORATE OUR FLOWER DRUM!

JENETTE.

IF I ENJOY BEING A GIRL

TED.

KISSING IN THE SHADOWS,

HEATHER.

PEOPLE WILL SAY,

JONATHAN.

"I TOLD YOU SO!"

TED.

IF I LOVED YOU,

JENETTE.

IT'S BECAUSE YOU'RE A WONDERFUL GUY.

MEN.

SHALL WE DANCE?

WOMEN.

YOU KNOW I CAN'T SAY "NO"!

ALL.

AS TWO YOUNG LOVERS WE'LL NEVER WALK
    ALONE.

MEN.

A FELLOW NEEDS TO HAVE A GIRL TO PLAY
    THIS GAME.

GIRLS.
WHAT'S THE USE OF WONDERIN', YOU'VE BEEN
    CAREFULLY TAUGHT:
MEN.
THERE IS NOTHING LIKE A DAME!
HEATHER.
DOE, MY DEAR, HOW MY HEART SINGS,
JONATHAN.
HONEY BUN, YOU'RE ONE OF MY FAV'RITE
    THINGS
ALL.
IN A RODGERS AND
H—A—M—M—E—R—S—T—E—I—N AFFAIR!

(*BLACKOUT, all leave adlibbing and bumping except* JENETTE
    who stops over by GABBY *and* DAN *who are ready for
    their next number.*)

JENETTE. (*In a dimmed "wing" area.*) No, Ted, I think they
really like you better. (*Pause.*) Ted?
DAN. I'm not Ted.
JENETTE. What number is this?
DAN. "Less is More and More."
JENETTE. Oh, excuse me, I'm sorry!

(DAN *and* GABBY *sing. Follow spot comes up on the two.*)

DAN.
I'VE GOT LOTS OF MONEY,
BUT LET ME TELL YOU, HONEY,
A LOT
IS NOT
ENOUGH ANYMORE!
GABBY.
IN A MILLION DOLLAR
APARTMENT LIVE-IN SQUALOR!
DAN.
FIFTH AVENUE
GABBY.
BESIDES THE VIEW
DAN and GABBY.
WE CAN AFFORD
THE ROOM BUT NOT BOARD.
DAN.
I'D LOVE TO BUY YOU LAMB CHOPS IF ONLY
    I COULD.

GABBY.
DARLING, READY MONEY IS THE ROOT OF
   ALL GOOD!
DAN.
JUST LEAVE YOUR BILLS OUTSIDE, AND COME
   AND HIDE
BEHIND MY DOOR,
SINCE LESS IS MORE AND MORE!
DAN.
IF I HAD THE COINAGE,
I'D KEEP YOU IN SIRLOINAGE.
BUT CASH FOR HASH
IS ALL THAT I HAVE.
GABBY.
WITH THE LEGAL TENDER
I'D BUY A WARING BLENDER,
DAN and GABBY.
BUT NOT THIS YEAR,
BELIEVE ME, DEAR,
WE AIN'T GOT THE BOB
FOR CORN ON THE COB.
DAN.
I'D LOVE TO BUY YOU BAGELS AND MAYBE
   SOME LOX,
BUT NOWADAYS THAT MEANS I'D HAVE TO
   RIP OFF FORT KNOX!
GABBY.
IT ONLY TAKES A GRAND
TO BUY A CAN
OF ALBACORE,
SINCE LESS IS MORE AND MORE!

DAN.
WITH A DOUBLE EAGLE
I'D MAKE OUR LOVING LEGAL
GABBY.
BUT SIN
IS IN
TILL PRICES GO DOWN.
DAN.
I'D RESORT TO ARSON
IF IT WOULD PAY THE PARSON!
DAN and GABBY.
TO SAY "I DO!"
AN I.O.U.

JUST WOULDN'T SUFFICE
WITHOUT ANY ICE.
    DAN.
SO SOMEDAY IN THE FUTURE I'LL ASK FOR
    YOUR HAND,
THEN YOU WILL BE WINED AND DINED AND
    MOO GOO GAI PANNED!
    DAN and GABBY.
BUT TILL WE HAVE A DIME
THAT IS THE TIME
WE'RE WAITING FOR
SINCE LESS IS MORE AND MORE!

(*BLACKOUT.*)

(*Follow spot up on* JENETTE *Center Stage.*)

    JENETTE.
WE HAD A HAPPY MARRIAGE, A BRIGHT
    DOMESTIC SCENE,
TILL SKIES BEGAN TO DARKEN AND
    SOMETHING CAME BETWEEN. . . .

I HATE FOOTBALL AND I FEEL I MUST REBEL
FOR MY HOME'S BEEN CONQUERED BY THE
    N.F.L.
I STAND IGNORED IN MY LOVELIEST
    NIGHTGOWN,
BECAUSE OUR TEAM HAS SCORED
OR MADE THEIR FOOL FIRST DOWN.
I HATE FOOTBALL!
THAT'S A FACT I GUARANTEE;
IF I HAD THE COURAGE, I'D SMASH OUR
    NEW T.V.
THE EVENING IS COOL; THERE IS PERFUME
    IN MY HAIR:
I FEEL LIKE A FOOL, ALL ALONE UPSTAIRS!

WHY IS IT SO ENTHRALLING?
THEY'VE GOT IT IN THEIR BLOOD,
TO WATCH THOSE MEN GO CRAWLING
AND ROLLING IN THE MUD!
THEY KEEP RIGHT ON PLAYING WHEN THE
    RAIN IS POURING.

WHY SUCH DEVOTION TO SOMETHING THAT'S
    SO BORING?

I HATE FOOTBALL!
I'LL NO LONGER PERSEVERE . . .
THEY'VE MADE THE SEASON LAST THE WHOLE
    DAMN YEAR.
THE SPRING AND THE SUMMER NO LONGER
    BRING RELIEF
FROM A COLT OR A COWBOY OR KANSAS CITY
    CHIEF!
TO DINING AND TO DANCING, I'LL SAY
    "GOODBYE"
CAUSE DOLPHINS GOTTA SWIM AND FALCONS
    GOTTA FLY!
CAN WE RECRUIT A CRUSADE OF RALPH
    NADER'S
TO SAVE THE POOR HOUSEWIFE FROM THE
    OAKLAND RAIDERS?
MY HUSBAND KNOWS EVERY REDSKIN BUT HE
    FORGETS MY NAME
AND TELLS ME TO BE QUIET, "IT'S TIME FOR
    THE GAME!"
I HATE IT!
OLÉ OLÉ
NO LAY!
I HATE IT!

(*BLACKOUT.* JENETTE *crosses to listen to* DAN *and* TED.)

DAN. The show's going pretty smoothly. Jonathan is doing
fine.
TED. That's onstage. Backstage he's going bananas.
JENETTE. Why?
TED. That new solo comes up in three numbers. He's afraid
he'll forget the words. (JENETTE *exits to offer help.*)
DAN. Oh.
TED. I told him not to worry . . . that he'd do fine.
DAN. Did it help?
TED. He tried to thank me but he couldn't remember my
name! (*BLACKOUT,* HEATHER *enters.*)
DAN. We're on.

(DAN *and* TED *become "backup boys" for* HEATHER's *number.*
    Spot up on HEATHER.)

HEATHER.
ONCE I LOVED TWO MEN, AND I KNEW I'D
    HAVE TO CHOOSE;
BUT I NEVER QUITE SUSPECTED HOW BADLY
    I WOULD LOSE.
I CALLED THEM BOTH TOGETHER AND SAID
    "NOW, WE'RE ALL ADULTS."
I EXPECTED THEY'D BE SHATTERED, BUT,
    WELL, HERE ARE THE RESULTS:
    (*Lights up to reveal men, posed at either side of stage.*)
THEY LEFT ME . . . FOR EACH OTHER.
SOLVED MY PROBLEM, NOW I'M FREE.
THEY LEFT ME . . . FOR EACH OTHER.
HOW UNCHIVALROUS FOR GENTLEMEN TO BE.

I HAD TOLD EACH ONE ABOUT THE OTHER
TO EXPLAIN MY DIVIDED LOYALTY.
I MUST HAVE BEEN VERY CONVINCING:
NOW THEY'VE BOTH FORGOTTEN ME!
    (*They wave surreptitiously and suddenly to each other,
    she catches them out of the corner of her eye.*)

THEY LEFT ME . . . FOR EACH OTHER.
I SHOULD FIND SOMEONE NEW.
IF ONLY THEY'D HAD A BROTHER,
BUT I GUESS THAT WOULDN'T WORK: THEY'D
    WANT HIM TOO!
IT'S QUITE PECULIAR
WITHOUT A DOUBT
HOW THIS TRIANGULAR RELATIONSHIP WORKED
    OUT!

(*Fade to BLACK. She exits,* DAN *and* TED *start the next
    number:*)

    DAN and TED. (*Lights up fast.*)
LET ME TELL YOU IT'S GREAT TO BE GAY,
GLAD THAT WE WENT ASTRAY!
    TED. (*They Charleston.*)
WE'VE NO REGRETS FOR WHAT WE'VE DONE.
    DAN.
WHO COULD THINK A MEN'S ROOM COULD BE
    SUCH FUN!?

    (*Enter* JENETTE, JONNY, *and* GABBY.)

BUT WE'VE ALL DUE RESPECTS
FOR THE OPPOSITE SEX;
THEY GIVE US A GOOD BASIS FOR COMPARISON
AND NO ONE SAYS WE EVER LEAVE OUT
    ANYONE!
    (*They see* JONATHAN *come in between* JENETTE *and*
    GABBY, *flirting.*)
COME ON ALONG!
    (*They sing to* JONATHAN.)
COME ON ALONG!
LET ME TAKE YOU BY THE HAND!
UP TO THE MAN,
UP TO THE MAN,
WHO'S THE BEST BOY IN THE BAND!
    JONATHAN.
I KNOW ALL ABOUT . . .
IT'S GREAT TO BE GAY,
IT'S UP, UP AND AWAY!
    (*The three men exit, hand in hand.*)

    GABBY. (*Cry of hurt surprise.*)
I ALWAYS THOUGHT HE ACTED JUST A BIT
    WITHDRAWN
    JENETTE.
BUT THERE'S SOMETHING THAT I'D LIKE TO
    TELL YOU NOW THAT HE'S GONE:

I THINK THAT IT'S GREAT TO BE GAY
PLEASE DON'T THINK I'M RISQUÉ.
    GABBY.
DON'T SAY ANOTHER WORD,
I MEAN, JUST TAKE IT EASY;
FOR AGES I'VE BEEN HOPING TO A-C YOUR D-C!
    (*The three men re-ener.*)

    ALL.
LET ME TELL YOU IT'S GREAT TO BE GAY
IN AN OUTSPOKEN WAY!
    HEATHER. (*Appears in the middle of the group. She sings:*)
FOR I'M IN LOVE WITH BARBARA WALTERS!
    ALL.
IN THE LIBERATED NATION CALLED THE
      U.S. OF A.,
IT'S GREAT TO BE GAY!
YEAH!

(*BLACKOUT. In blackout, *JONATHAN* loosens his vest velcro
    so it appears to be torn and hanging down. He shows*
    HEATHER.)

JONATHAN. Look, my vest just tore, and my new number's
coming up!
    HEATHER. Hurry backstage . . . I'll fix it. (JONNY *and*
HEATHER *exit. *DAN *and *TED *have not noticed this, they are off
in wings.*)
    TED. Well, it's almost over. (*Empty spotlight appears Stage
Center back wall.*)
    DAN. No major foul ups.
    TED. Why is there no one in that spotlight?
    DAN. Where's Jonathan? (*Panic.*)
    GABBY. Jonny's costume fell apart; Heather's pinning him!
    DAN. Somebody do something!
    JENETTE. Do a number!
    TED. There *are* no more numbers!
    JENETTE. "Less is More and More" . . . do the verse they
cut out!
    DAN. I can't!
    GABBY. I won't remember it!
    TED. You're on!

(*Spotlight up full—*GABBY *and *DAN *are pushed into spotlight.*)

    DAN.
IF I HAD A QUARTER,
WE'D RAISE A BABY DAUGHTER.
    GABBY.
BUT SHE
    (*Very halting choreography is performed.*)
WOULD BE A BIT UNDERED!
    DAN.
BABIES COST A SHEKEL
FOR EACH AND EVERY FRECKLE.
    GABBY.
WITHOUT SOME CHIPS
SHE'D TAKE NO TRIPS,
    DAN *and *GABBY.
A PLANE TO PERU
COSTS MORE THAN A SOU.
    DAN.
DARLING, IF YOU REALLY WANT A BURGER
    OR FRANK,

I'LL RUSH DOWN TO WALL STREET NOW AND
    HOLD UP A BANK!
    DAN and GABBY.
NOW WE CAN'T SEE THE TOWN WITHOUT
    A CROWN
OR LOUIS D'OR,
SINCE LESS IS MORE AND MORE!

    JENETTE. (*Pokes head out from wings.*) He's not ready yet!
Do another verse!

    DAN. (*Through clenched teeth and big smile.*) There *are*
no more verses.

    JENETTE. Well, make one up! (*Disappears!*)

    DAN. (*Still through clenched teeth.*) What's another kind of
money?

    GABBY. Pesetas?

    DAN. (*Sings.*)
IF I HAD PESETAS . . .
    (*Squeezes* GABBY.)
    GABBY.
I'D WOO YOU WITH TOMATOES,
    DAN.
BUT NO MORE DOUGH MY PIGGY JUST SAID.
    GABBY.
IF I HAD A DUCAT
WE THEN CAN . . . UH . . . (*Very fast.*) SEARS
    ROEBUCK IT!
AND GIVE MY KALE
TO BLOOMINGDALE . . .
    DAN.
AND SHELL OUT A ROLL
FOR FILET OF SOLE!
    GABBY.
NOW JUST THE BARE ESSENTIALS COST A
    MIGHTY BIG SUM . . .
    DAN.
I'LL SPOIL ALL THE REST OF YOU EXCEPT FOR
    YOUR TUM . . . MY.
STAY WITH ME TONIGHT
AND THEN THIS PLIGHT
    (GABBY *starts giggling.*)
WE CAN IGNORE
    DAN and GABBY.
SINCE LESS IS MORE AND MORE . . .

    JENETTE. Not yet!

    GABBY. Oh, please!

DAN and GABBY.
LESS IS MORE AND MORE . . .
    JENETTE. He's ready! (JONATHAN *runs by them to his place by the piano.*)
    DAN and GABBY.
LESS IS MORE AND MORE!
    DAN. Thank God!

    JONATHAN. (*After running across stage. Spotlight up fast. Chanted.*)

WE'RE ACTORS,
AND THERE'RE PEOPLE WHO THINK
WE MUST TAKE DRUGS OR DRINK
AND WE MEET FOR AN ORGY EACH DAY . . .
    GABBY.
AND I CAN'T MAKE AMENDS
TO MY MOTHER'S BEST FRIENDS
WHO ALL THINK I LIVE EACH ROLE I PLAY!
    JONATHAN.
AT TIMES WE MAY RUE IT
    GABBY.
AND WHY DO WE DO IT?
    JONATHAN.
IN ANSWER I'D JUST HAVE TO SAY:
    (*Sung:*)
I'LL DIE IF I CAN'T LIVE FOREVER,
IF ONLY MY FRIENDS KNOW MY NAME.
I'LL DIE IF I CAN'T LIVE FOREVER,
AND NOT KNOW THE FEELING OF FAME!

I'LL DIE IF I CAN'T LIVE FOREVER,
IF I CAN'T LEAVE A MARK WHERE I'VE BEEN!
I HOPE THAT I WON'T BE FORGOTTEN
AT THE END OF EACH SHOW THAT I'M IN!
    GABBY.
I'M ALWAYS HOPING THAT I
WILL HEAR SOMEONE QUOTE
FROM A SONG THAT I WROTE;
IF I CAN'T LIVE FOREVER I'LL DIE!

    (*Enter* JENETTE *and* HEATHER, *lights up to half.*)

    JENETTE and HEATHER.
FOR EIGHT SHOWS A WEEK WE'LL KEEP
    SMILING,
AND SEEKING SOME MEANS TO ADVANCE.

ALL.
OUR RESUME CREDITS COMPILING
CAUSE WE'RE YOUNG AND WE THINK WE'VE
    A CHANCE,
GOT A CHANCE, GOT A CHANCE!
    (*Enter* TED *and* DAN, *lights up full.*)
I'LL DIE IF I CAN'T LIVE FOREVER,
IF ONLY MY FRIENDS KNOW MY NAME.
I'LL DIE IF I CAN'T LIVE FOREVER
AND NOT KNOW THE FEELING OF FAME.

I'LL DIE IF I CAN'T LIVE FOREVER,
PLEASE SPARE US ONE MOMENT OF FAME.
I'LL DIE IF I CAN'T LIVE FOREVER . . .
SO PLEASE, PLEASE, REMEMBER
MY NAME, MY NAME, MY NAME, MY NAME!

(*BLACKOUT.*)

(*All rush to same positions as in beginning of opening number
    and sing to same tune: Lights up fast.*)

ALL.
IT'S THE FINALE,
IT'S THE FINALE!
BECAUSE THE SHOW IS JUST ABOUT OVER.
THE SHOW IS FINISHED NOW,
IT'S TIME TO TAKE A BOW,
WHICH WE WILL DO BECAUSE
WE HOPE TO HEAR APPLAUSE!
    (*Pause.*)
THIS IS THE END OF THE,
IS THE END OF THE
    (*All bow to musical interlude.*)
BECAUSE THIS IS THE END OF THE SHOW!
    (*They exit.*)

(*Fade to BLACK. This is the end of the revue within the
    revue. They rush off and get their first act hats and coats
    that went with the characters and put them on over their
    evening dress and come out for the encore: Lights up.
    Enter* DAN, HEATHER, *and* JENETTE.)

HEATHER.
NO ONE EVER TOLD ME WHAT A FUTURE I'D
    ENGAGE
WHEN I LET MY MOTHER PUT HER DAUGHTER
    ON THE STAGE!

I CAN PERFORM ON CUE ANYTIME AND
    ANYWHERE.
YOU NEVER KNOW WHO'S WATCHING: A
    PRODUCER MIGHT BE THERE!
JENETTE.
I'VE TRIED TO FIND A JOB; MY AUDITION IS
    REHEARSED:
BUT EVERYWHERE I GO TEN THOUSAND
    OTHERS GET THERE FIRST!
DAN.
IT'S GREAT WHEN YOU ARE WORKING, BUT
    EACH ACTOR SEEMS TO KNOW:
YOU MAKE MUCH MORE ON WELFARE THAN
    THEY PAY YOU FOR A SHOW!
THEN AFTER TWENTY SEVEN TRYOUTS YOU
    ARE CAST . . .
JENETTE.
THE OPENING PERFORMANCE IS THE FIRST
    AND IT'S THE LAST!
    (Others enter.)
ALL.
BUT IT'S A JOY, JUST A JOY (YOU CAN'T
    IMAGINE)
WHEN YOU WALK THE GREAT WHITE WAY.

GABBY.
I DANCE AND ACT OR SING EVERY SONG THAT
    I COMPOSE;
BUT ALL THEY WANT TO KNOW IS HOW I LOOK
    WITHOUT MY CLOTHES!
JONATHAN.
THE OTHER ACTORS THAT YOU MAY MEET JUST
    PROVE AGAIN
THAT GIRLS AREN'T ALWAYS GIRLS AND ALL
    THE BOYS MAY NOT BE MEN!
HEATHER.
DIRECTORS MAKE YOU OFFERS WHICH NO
    STRUGGLING GIRL COULD SCOFF:

THEY PROMISE YOU "OFF-BROADWAY" BUT
    YOU FIND IT'S "OFF OFF OFF!"
    TED.
YOU MUST BE CAREFUL WHEN YOU SHARE
    A DRESSING ROOM . . .
WHERE WOULD BE THE SAFEST BECAUSE
    WHICH DOES WHAT TO WHOM?
    ALL.
BUT IT'S A JOY, JUST A JOY (YOU CAN'T
    IMAGINE)
WHEN YOU WALK THE GREAT WHITE WAY.
    DAN.
AND THOUGH AT FIRST YOU'RE SODA JERKING,
    GABBY.
VERY SOON YOU MAY BE WORKING!
    JENETTE.
AND YOU'LL TAKE MORE BOWS THAN "HELLO
    DOLLY" COULD!
    HEATHER.
AND THE PHOTOGRAPHERS ARE GRINNING,
    JONATHAN.
WITH SUCCESS YOUR HEAD IS SPINNING,
    TED.
AND YOU'RE PACKING UP TO MOVE TO
    HOLLYWOOD!
    ALL.
OO—OO—OO—WAH!
    DAN. (*Shouted as all throw hats up and back.*) Mary Tyler
Moore here we come!

    ALL.
WE'D NEVER LEAVE THIS LIFE WITH ITS TINSEL
    AND ITS GAUZE
WHO CARES IF YOU ARE STARVING IF EACH
    NIGHT YOU HEAR APPLAUSE!
    HEATHER.
IN DINNER THEATRE DAYS, I WOULD NEVER
    MISS A CUE . . .
    DAN.
WHILE BUSBOYS BROKE THE DISHES AND I
    SLIPPED ON BITS OF STEW!
    JONATHAN.
REMEMBER OUTDOOR DRAMA . . . ALL THOSE
    SUMMERS IN THE SOUTH . . .

TED.
RECITING LOFTY SPEECHES WHILE THE BUGS
  FLEW IN YOUR MOUTH!
GABBY and JENETTE.
YOU'LL SOON FORGET THE NASTY PEOPLE AND
  THE FIGHTS . . .
ALL.
THAT CAME BEFORE THE MOMENT WHEN YOU
  SEE YOUR NAME IN LIGHTS.
BUT IT'S A JOY, JUST A JOY (YOU CAN'T
  IMAGINE)
WHEN YOU WALK THE GREAT WHITE WAY!

(*BLACKOUT and Curtain Calls.*)

END

PROPERTY LIST

1 guitar without strings
1 casette tape recorder with strap
1 pre-recorded casette for "A IS FOR" number
1 country-western "Minnie Pearl" hat
1 feather boa for "Walter Cronkite" number
6 adding machine tape rolls with names of Congress for "Who Do We Thank?"
1 small suitcase for Jonathan's first number and apartment sketch
2 umbrellas for "My Life's A Musical Comedy"
6 theater trade newspapers: BACKSTAGE and SHOW BUSINESS
assorted sheet music and audition gear (Pix, resumes, purses)
5 chairlike letters spelling "R E V U E"
1 cymbal for "crash" in offstage rehearsal scene
1 tennis shoe to sniff in "Where Would We Be Without Perverts?"
2 "Win" buttons for "Less is More and More"
6 hats to throw on "Mary Tyler Moore" line in "The Great White Way"
6 coats for "Perverts" number

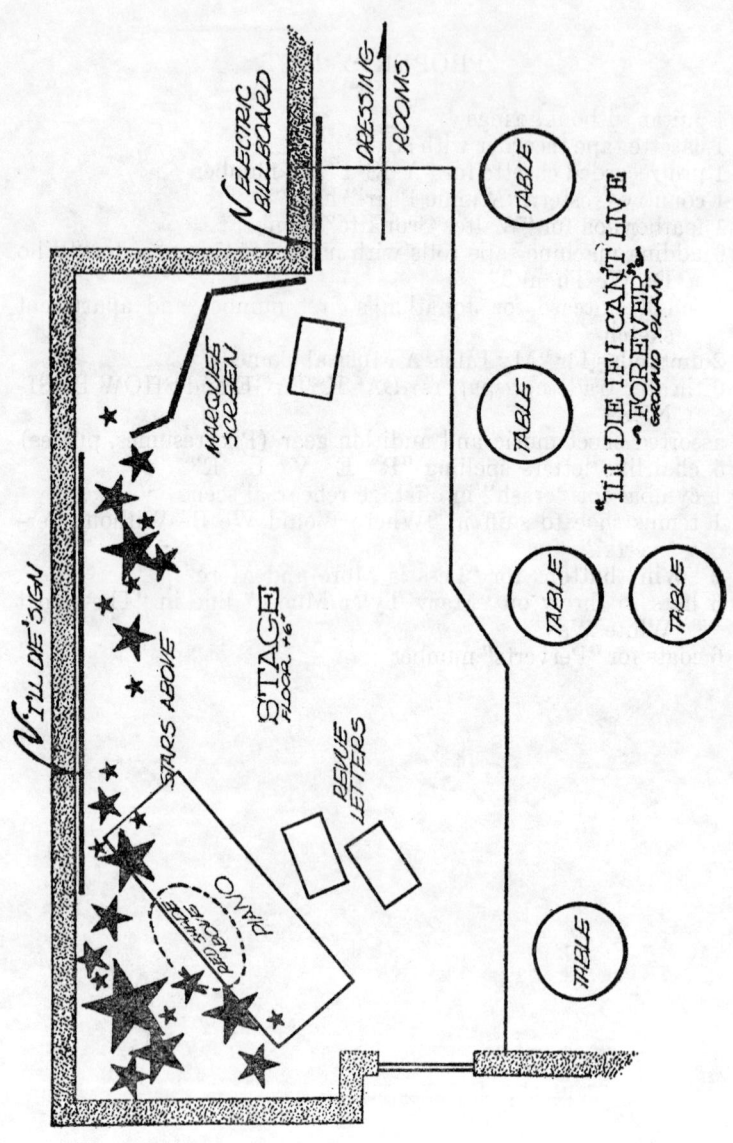

"I'LL DIE IF I CAN'T LIVE FOREVER"
GROUND PLAN

60

6 RMS RIV VU
BOB RANDALL

(Little Theatre) Comedy
4 Men, 4 Women, Interior

A vacant apartment with a river view is open for inspection by prospective tenants, and among them are a man and a woman who have never met before. They are the last to leave and, when they get ready to depart, they find that the door is locked and they are shut in. Since they are attractive young people, they find each other interesting and the fact that both are happily married adds to their delight of mutual, yet obviously separate interests.

"... a Broadway comedy of fun and class, as cheerful as a rising souffle. A sprightly, happy comedy of charm and humor. Two people playing out a very vital game of love, an attractive fantasy with a precious tincture of truth to it."— *N.Y. Times.*
"... perfectly charming entertainment, sexy, romantic and funny."—*Women's Wear Daily.*

Royalty, $50–$35

WHO KILLED SANTA CLAUS?
TERENCE FEELY

(All Groups) Thriller
6 Men, 2 Women, Interior

Barbara Love is a popular television 'auntie'. It is Christmas, and a number of men connected with her are coming to a party. Her secretary, Connie, is also there. Before they arrive she is threatened by a disguised voice on her Ansaphone, and is sent a grotesque 'murdered' doll in a coffin, wearing a dress resembling one of her own. She calls the police, and a handsome detective arrives. Shortly afterwards her guests follow. It becomes apparent that one of those guests is planning to kill her. Or is it the strange young man who turns up unexpectedly, claiming to belong to the publicity department, but unknown to any of the others?

"... is a thriller with heaps of suspense, surprises, and nattily cleaver turns and twists ... Mr. Feeley is technically highly skilled in the artificial range of operations, and his dialogue is brilliantly effective."—The Stage. London.

Royalty, $50–$25

THE SEA HORSE
EDWARD J. MOORE

(Little Theatre) Drama
I Man, I Woman, Interior

It is a play that is, by turns, tender, ribald, funny and suspenseful. Audiences everywhere will take it to their hearts because it is touched with humanity and illuminates with glowing sympathy the complexities of a man-woman relationship. Set in a West Coast waterfront bar, the play is about Harry Bales, a seaman, who, when on shore leave, usually heads for "The Sea Horse," the bar run by Gertrude Blum, the heavy, unsentimental proprietor. Their relationship is purely physical and, as the play begins, they have never confided their private yearnings to each other. But this time Harry has returned with a dream: to buy a charter fishing boat and to have a son by Gertrude. She, in her turn, has made her life one of hard work, by day, and nocturnal love-making; she has encased her heart behind a facade of toughness, utterly devoid of sentimentality, because of a failed marriage. Irwin's play consists in the ritual of "dance" courtship by Harry of Gertrude, as these two outwardly abrasive characters fight, make up, fight again, spin dreams, deflate them, make love and reveal their long locked-up secrets.

"A burst of brilliance!"—*N.Y. Post.* "I was touched close to tears!"—*Village Voice.* "A must! An incredible love story. A beautiful play!"—*Newhouse Newspapers.* "A major new playwright!"—*Variety.*
Copies late fall. ROYALTY, $50–$35

THE AU PAIR MAN
HUGH LEONARD

(Little Theatre) Comedy
I Man, I Woman, Interior

The play concerns a rough Irish bill collector named Hartigan, who becomes a love slave and companion to an English lady named Elizabeth, who lives in a cluttered London town house, which looks more like a museum for a British Empire on which the sun has long set. Even the door bell chimes out the national anthem. Hartigan is immediately conscripted into her service in return for which she agrees to teach him how to be a gentleman rather after the fashion of a reverse Pygmalion. The play is a wild one, and is really the never-ending battle between England and Ireland. Produced to critical acclaim at Lincoln Center's Vivian Beaumont Theatre.

ROYALTY, $50–$35

A Breeze from The Gulf

MART CROWLEY

(Little Theatre) Drama

The author of "The Boys in the Band" takes us on a journey back to a small Mississippi town to watch a 15-year-old boy suffer through adolescence to adulthood and success as a writer. His mother is a frilly southern doll who has nothing to fall back on when her beauty fades. She develops headaches and other physical problems, while the asthmatic son turns to dolls and toys at an age when other boys are turning to sports. The traveling father becomes withdrawn, takes to drink; and mother takes to drugs to kill the pain of the remembrances of things past. She eventually ends in an asylum, and the father in his fumbling way tries to tell the son to live the life he must.

"The boy is plunged into a world of suffering he didn't create. . . . One of the most electrifying plays I've seen in the past few years . . . Scenes boil and hiss . . . The dialogue goes straight to the heart." Reed, **Sunday News.**

Royalty, $50–$35

ECHOES

N. RICHARD NASH

(All Groups) Drama

2 Men, 1 Woman, Interior

A young man and woman build a low-keyed paradise of happiness within an asylum, only to have it shattered by the intrusion of the outside world. The two characters search, at times agonizingly to determine the difference between illusion and reality. The effort is lightened at times by moments of shared love and "pretend" games, like decorating Christmas trees that are not really there. The theme of love, vulnerable to the surveillances of the asylum, and the ministrations of the psychiatrist, (a non-speaking part) seems as fragile in the constrained setting as it often is in the outside world.

". . . even with the tragic, sombre theme there is a note of hope and possible release and the situations presented specifically also have universal applications to give it strong effect . . . intellectual, but charged with emotion."—**Reed.**

Royalty, $50–$35

VERONICA'S ROOM
IRA LEVIN
(Little Theatre) Mystery
2 Men, 2 Women, Interior

VERONICA'S ROOM is, in the words of one reviewer, "a chew-up-your-finger-nails thriller-chiller" in which "reality and fantasy are entwined in a totally absorbing spider web of who's-doing-what-to-whom." The heroine of the play is 20-year-old Susan Kerner, a Boston University student who, while dining in a restaurant with Larry Eastwood, a young lawyer, is accosted by a charming elderly Irish couple, Maureen and John Mackey (played on Broadway by Eileen Heckart and Arthur Kennedy). These two are overwhelmed by Susan's almost identical resemblance to Veronica Brabissant, a long-dead daughter of the family for whom they work. Susan and Larry accompany the Mackeys to the Brabissant mansion to see a picture of Veronica, and there, in Veronica's room, which has been preserved as a shrine to her memory, Susan is induced to impersonate Veronica for a few minutes in order to solace the only surviving Brabissant, Veronica's addled sister who lives in the past and believes that Veronica is alive and angry with her. "Just say you're not angry with her," Mrs. Mackey instructs Susan. "It'll be such a blessin' for her!" But once Susan is dressed in Veronica's clothes, and Larry has been escorted downstairs by the Mackeys, Susan finds herself locked in the room and locked in the role of Veronica. Or is she really Veronica, in the year 1935, pretending to be an imaginary Susan?

The play's twists and turns are, in the words of another critic, "like finding yourself trapped in someone else's nightmare," and "the climax is as jarring as it is surprising." "Neat and elegant thriller."—*Village Voice*.

ROYALTY, $50–$35

MY FAT FRIEND
CHARLES LAURENCE
(Little Theatre) Comedy
3 Men, 1 Woman, Interior

Vicky, who runs a bookshop in Hampstead, is a heavyweight. Inevitably she suffers, good-humouredly enough, the slings and arrows of the two characters who share the flat over the shop; a somewhat glum Scottish youth who works in an au pair capacity, and her lodger, a not-so-young homosexual. When a customer—a handsome bronzed man of thirty—seems attracted to her she resolves she will slim by hook or by crook. Aided by her two friends, hard exercise, diet and a graph, she manages to reduce to a stream-lined version of her former self—only to find that it was her rotundity that attracted the handsome book-buyer in the first place. When, on his return, he finds himself confronted by a sylph his disappointment is only too apparent. The newly slim Vicky is left alone once more, to be consoled (up to a point) by her effeminate lodger.

"My fat Friend is abundant with laughs."—*Times Newsmagazine*. "If you want to laugh go."—*WCBS-TV*.

ROYALTY, $50–$35

#5